WORSHIP EXPERIENCES

Jim Burns and Robin Dugall

GENERAL
EDITOR

AUTHOR

Gospel Light

Gospel Light is an evangelical Christian publisher dedicated to serving the local church. We believe God's vision for Gospel Light is to provide church leaders with biblical, user-friendly materials that will help them evangelize, disciple and minister to children, youth and families.

We hope this Gospel Light resource will help you discover biblical truth for your own life and help you minister to youth. God bless you in your work.

For a free catalog of resources from Gospel Light please contact your Christian supplier or contact us at 1-800-4-GOSPEL *or* www.gospellight.com.

PUBLISHING STAFF
William T. Greig, Publisher
Dr. Elmer L. Towns, Senior Consulting Publisher
Dr. Gary S. Greig, Senior Consulting Editor
Pam Weston, Editor
Patti Virtue, Assistant Editor
Christi Goeser, Editorial Assistant
Kyle Duncan, Associate Publisher
Bayard Taylor, M.Div., Senior Editor, Theological and Biblical Issues
Kevin Parks, Cover Designer
Debi Thayer, Designer

ISBN 0-8307-2404-4
© 1999 by Jim Burns
All rights reserved.
Printed in U.S.A.

HOW TO MAKE CLEAN COPIES FROM THIS BOOK

Contents

Contents

Dedication

I dedicate this writing to the people who have made the most profound impact on my worship life: the ministry of Calvary Chapel and Maranatha Music, Vineyard Church and the late John Wimber's ministry, Hillsongs Music in Australia, and especially my wife, Vicky S. Dugall, and the countless worship leaders who have sung, prayed and led with me over the years, including my friends in the worship and praise ministry at Good Shepherd Lutheran Church in Irvine, California, with whom I currently serve the Lord.

I also thank the people who affirmed the gifts God so graciously gave me and helped launch a ministry in my life that I still count as an honor and privilege: Jim Burns, Jim Hale, Tom Ashbrook, T. J. Anderson, Kevin Murphy, Paul Westerhoff, Bill Crouser, Bob St. Clair, and the numerous students and Christian friends who have stood side by side with me before the Lord. I can't wait until we are together in heaven, praising God forever. What a joy that will be!

—Robin Dugall

Introduction

So you're a youth worker! Congratulations! You are called by God to do the most vital ministry in the Body of Christ: training, equipping, discipling and leading young Christians into effective and faithful service for Jesus Christ. Of all the ministry you do on a regular basis, there is none more important than worship. That might come as a surprise to you because expertise and experience in leading and teaching worship is not the first thing that the senior pastor expects from the average youth worker. You have camps, Bible studies, activities, trips, counseling and just "hanging" with students to do. Yet of all the treasures you can pass on to students who are eager to follow and please the heart of God, the *best* is a passion for worship. Your students may soon forget the games and crowd breakers that entertain them today, but they will not forget the spiritual depth that you help them plumb through spirit-to-Spirit encounters with the Lord of lords and King of kings.

My objective is very simple—to give you a workbook on how to put together worship experiences that allow God to move among the hearts and lives of today's students. This book was not easy to write simply because there is no programming of the Spirit of God. We can design youth ministry activities that have a high certainty of succeeding. We can say "This game is going to work, guaranteed" or "This method of Bible study will be a blessing to your students." We cannot do that with worship. If we did, we would be making a mockery of the essence of worship, that is, that worship at the core is a face-to-face meeting between believers and God, and you cannot program that! To paraphrase John 3:8: the Spirit blows where it pleases. I do not believe we can control the Spirit of God; the Spirit controls us. We have to discover ways to cooperate with the fresh wind of the Spirit in our midst. In other words, what can we do to catch the next "breeze" the Spirit blows near us? How can we put together experiences that give the Spirit of God opportunity to visit us and lovingly encounter our lives? Our excursion through this book will be just that, a journey. Please join me!

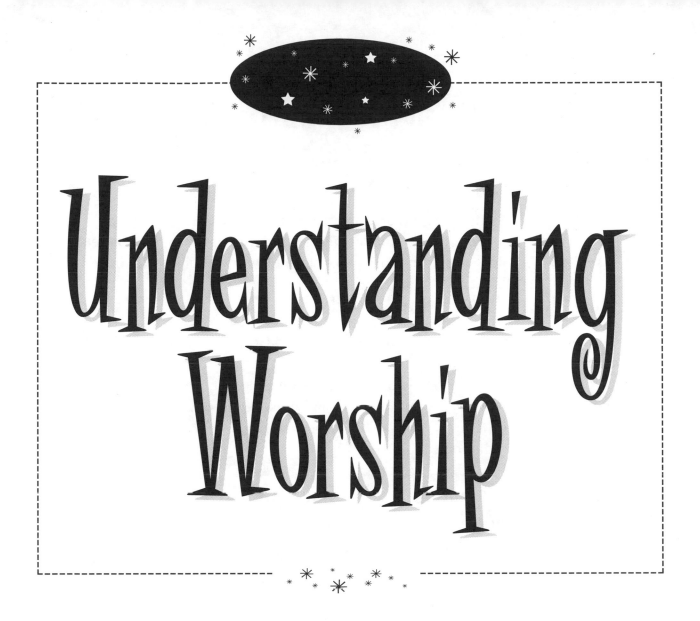

Understanding Worship

You want to lead worship? Prepare yourself! What worthwhile activity doesn't take preparation? The Boy Scouts had it down years ago when they declared very simply, "Be prepared." How do you prepare for worship? You prepare *you*!

What Worship *Is*

Worship *Is* Foundational

Worship is the foundation to the life of every believer in Jesus Christ. Worship is not an add-on or dispensable. We don't do worship just because we have nothing better to do. Being a spirited worshiper should be the goal of every Christian's life. Is it yours?

Worship *Is* a Meeting of Hearts

Worship is where your heart, your students' hearts and God's heart meet. Plain and simple, worship is an encounter with the creator of the universe. Psalm 22:3 says, "Yet you are enthroned as the Holy One; you are the praise of Israel." Imagine God visiting you face-to-face. Imagine what it must have been like to be Joseph, Mary, Moses or Paul. They didn't have to come up with plans to meet with God; God orchestrated that! He made it happen and it changed their lives.

Worship *Is* a Conscious Expression of Submission to God

Big words, but it is a very important concept for someone planning worship experiences to understand. When you evaluate the effectiveness of a worship experience, you don't just do it by how you or your students "feel"; you evaluate its long-range effectiveness by whether worship brings students closer to Jesus and more devoted to following Him in their daily lives.

Worship *Is* an Entry into Another World

Maybe you feel like your students are already from "another world." That's not what we're driving at here. We enter into God's presence through worship and enter into the rule of God. Worship gives us a chance to take a step into the kingdom of God.

   Now, think about what you know about the Bible. What happened when Jesus brought the reality of the kingdom of God into people's lives? People were touched; bodies and spirits were healed; salvation occurred; lives were transformed. What does that mean for you and your students? You want something big to chew on? Let's talk consequences. (**Note:** See the Bible study on "The Consequences of Worship" pp. 81-86). That's right—there are consequences to worship. There's power in worship. Meet that power—the Spirit of God—and you're bound to walk away a different person. What are some consequences? The Bible tells us there's salvation, deliverance, anointing for ministry and unity—and that's only the beginning!

Worship *Is* an Expression of Love

The best worship is uncomplicated. It is simply an articulation of love. Psalm 18:1 says, "I love you, O LORD." Jesus told us we now have the freedom to say "I love you, Lord" (see Mark 12:33). We don't have a relationship with God that is framed in formality. We can come with confidence into the presence of God. And more than that, this is our "*Abba*" (see Mark 14:36; that's an expression of parental intimacy in the New Testament). Jesus can't wait to have you in His presence.

Someone once told me that if the Lord carried a wallet, He would have our pictures in it. Jesus is crazy about you and your students. We seek in worship to build a sense of love between our students and God. How do we do that? How do you fall in love with someone? You get to know them; you focus on who they are and how they touch your life in deep and meaningful ways. Nurture a sense of love for the Lord God. With all the superficiality of love in our modern world, students need to know what real love is! God is love!

Worship *Is* a Lifestyle

Worship is not restricted to any one time or place. We are called by God to be worshipers in every area and time in our lives. Be an example to students of worship as a lifestyle choice for you. Don't have your worship life be limited to what you do at church. Tell stories of how worship touches your life and theirs all the time. Students are looking for a role model—someone to emulate and to teach them what it means to be a growing Christian. Allow them to imitate you when it comes to worship. If you think about it, we all learn by imitating others. Teach them that worship is something that Jesus said should be done "in spirit and in truth" (John 4:24). Worship is "whatever you do, whether in word or deed, do it all in the name of the Lord Jesus, giving thanks to God the Father through him" (Colossians 3:17).

Some Thoughts Concerning Worship

The dictionary gives us another definition of worship. It means to "serve a superior."[1] God is our superior. He is the One we serve with all of our lives. 1 Peter 5:6 encourages all to "Humble yourselves, therefore, under God's mighty hand, that he may lift you up in due time." Humbling ourselves is an act of worship. It puts us in a place where we have to ask, "Who am I really serving? Who is really the Lord of my life? What is my humility quotient?" Self-examination in this manner is not only a part of the worship experience, but also a portion of what God wants to do in and through us as we worship.

We don't go to worship—God comes to us. The Bible says that God makes worship happen by inhabiting the praises of His people (see Psalm 22:3). Worship humbles the proud and lifts up the humble.

Worship should involve all of our emotions and feelings. In other words, there are no feeling or emotional rules about what you should or should not feel during worship. The Bible says we can feel joy, sadness, regret, ecstasy, peace and a myriad of other feelings when God touches our lives.

Galatians 6:7 says, "A man reaps what he sows." When it comes to worship, if you and your students expect God to be present and bless you in and through worship, guess what will happen? Be expectant! Don't approach worship in a cavalier manner; nobody in the Bible was ever praised for having a casual relationship with God. In other words, when it comes to worship, just do it— but do it with reverence!

Expect worship to build a sense of community among you and your students. Colossians 3:14-16 tells us that worship builds unity. Do you see love grow among students as you worship together?

Worship involves a sacrifice. The Bible says that sacrifice is us! (See Romans 12:1.) As we give ourselves to God, He'll give Himself to us!

What Worship Is *Not*

Worship Is *Not* Merely an Order of Service or a Liturgy

Worship is an encounter with the living God. An order of service is merely a means to an end. Everything that we do to design worship experiences is a vehicle to get students into the Lord's presence. Worship happens in their hearts. That means if you prefer more of a traditional slant on worship, that's okay. If you do contemporary worship, that is fine, too; but remember, your way is not the *only* way. All songs, readings, prayers, liturgies and hymns are instruments that enable us to enter God's presence.

Worship Is *Not* Owned by Any One Denomination

If you are Baptist, Lutheran, Presbyterian, Assembly of God, nondenominational or whatever, remember, you don't have the corner on effective worship. Understand this: We are all Christians. Whether we call ourselves Lutherans, Baptists or Methodists, we are just describing what "brand" of Christian we are. Secondly, we are in denominations based upon a uniformity of preference. In other words, you get a bunch of Christians together who agree on worship practice, doctrine, devotion to God, etc. and you have a denomination. What we're driving at is that there is much more to Christian worship than just what happens in *your* church. Your church might do worship really well. That's great! Praise the Lord for that! But other Christians worship God too. That's right! You might be able to learn something from them. Here's a sobering truth—God isn't interested in good Presbyterian, good Baptist or good charismatic worship; He desires worship that is sincere, life-changing, community-building and heart-encountering. Here's a suggestion: Visit other churches. See how they worship. Learn what you can. Look at how they enter God's presence. Incorporate some of their ideas. It will not only give you a sense of unity with other believers, but also a foretaste of something we are all going to enjoy for eternity—each other's presence as we worship God together!

Worship Is *Not* a Performance

Just because you might not "do" worship well, doesn't mean it is not effective in your life or your students' lives. Just because you might not have the best worship band or leader, doesn't mean the worship experiences of your students will be bankrupt. Yes, we want to do all with excellence. Yes, we serve and love an excellent God who would not want us to bring the leftovers of our efforts in praising Him. Yet sometimes we are so worried about performance that we simply can't let go and worship the Lord.

Do your best with the gifts and resources God has given you. Don't be envious of what another church has; just be yourself! Other ministries might not have the same tender heart you do. They might not have students who are ready to come into God's presence in the way your students are. God isn't impressed with the stuff of worship; He *is* impressed with lives that are available to Him. We can all do that!

Prepare Yourself

Be a Worshiper Yourself

Take worship seriously. Watch other worship leaders that you admire and respect. Spend time daily in worship. Students can sense whether their leaders are people who enjoy the refreshing presence of God. Students are tuned in to sincerity and authenticity. They will know. But most importantly, you *need* a vibrant and consistent worship life. Ministry takes it out on your heart, emotions and spirituality. Worship is like coming to a well of water and taking a huge drink. It refreshes you. It is the Gatorade of ministry. You need doses of God's presence in worship. You will be tempted to invest all your time in all the stuff that is required of you in ministry. We've all been there. But I'll tell you something that veterans in ministry know—you will not be able to minister with effectiveness with a heart that is shriveled up because of the demands and drain of ministry. Worship builds hearts, most especially yours!

Read about worship. See the "Suggested Reading" at the back of this book (pp. 115-117) for ideas. Be part of worship at your church. Show students that you not only support your church's ministry but that you need worship in your own life. Students are looking for an example or a model to emulate. Remember, many students do not have parents who take worship seriously. If you and your team of leaders demonstrate with lives that are tender and eager to worship, you will do your students a lifelong service.

A critical view of your church services only hurts students in the end. You might have a negative opinion of the services at the church where you minister. You might like the worship experiences at other churches better, but the church where you are serving the Lord is your students' church. They might not have the opportunities you do to worship in other places. If you take shots at the worship in your church, it will rub off on students. Are they apathetic about the worship of the church? Look at yourself first before you criticize them for not desiring worship the way you believe they should. Build up the worship of your church. Talk to the pastor about how the church might be more sensitive to the worship needs of students. Remember, the key to success in youth ministry isn't just what you see in students' lives today. If your students are active, growing and fruitful Christians in the church 10 years from now, then you can praise God for success. Build up your church's worship!

Look at Your Motives

Many worship leaders I have met are frustrated musicians or performers who simply want to get up in front of people for the sake of a personal affirmation. Your personal humility in worship leadership is a must. My experience tells me that when I am most proud or focused on myself, worship doesn't happen. Try to be as transparent as possible when you lead your students in worship. Don't allow them to focus on you but on Jesus. Remember the words of John the Baptist, "He must increase, but I must decrease"(John 3:30, *NKJV*). It might be good to write that verse on your guitar case, Bible cover, worship planning folder—everywhere! It will keep your motives pure.

Quick Tips on Worship Leadership

Be prepared. Take the worship time seriously enough to:

• Pray *about* it—come before the Lord for guidance;

• Prepare *for* it—don't just "wing" it. Prepare for worship as you would prepare for any significant ministry activity. Prepare yourself spiritually, scripturally and musically. Be ready to stand before people and present them with the best you can give as you lead them to the Lord; and

• Train leaders to lead it—develop worship teams with designated leaders. Team worship multiplies your ministry's effectiveness and fruitfulness with students over the long haul. It provides more active role models of sincere worshipers in your ministry.

Have a set practice time for the worship team. If you have more than one team, have each team practice the week before their turn.

Don't overwhelm students with too many new songs. Have a new song strategy. I try not to introduce more than two or three new songs a month to the congregation I serve. The point of worship music is to get people away from the words and melody and to focus on Jesus. Too many new songs will focus your worship strategy on trying to learn new words rather than on Jesus!

As with all good forms of communication, *use good eye contact and voice inflections when you lead.* You might even want to memorize the section of the Bible you are using to make the worship flow more effectively. The less fumbling between resources, the better.

Keep the worship flowing smoothly. Now, I have to admit, this is extremely subjective. What might make good worship for me might be different from you. What I mean by "flow" is this: How is the worship time moving? Are songs, prayers, readings and other worship experiences unnecessarily broken up by uncomfortable pauses or musical key changes? Are worship-filled lives interrupted as the leaders look for the next overhead transparency or fumble between song sheets? Any good worship time has a distinct flow to it. Ask someone in your group to help you evaluate when worship times are working and when they are derailed. What causes them to derail? What makes worship work in your group?

CHARACTERISTICS OF GOOD WORSHIP FLOW

- Provide smooth transitions between worship songs.
- Carefully plan key changes between songs. Don't have too many key changes.
- Have minimal interruptions between different aspects of worship (i.e., readings, prayers, songs, etc.).
- Allow very few moments of silence unless the silence is being utilized by the worship leader for prayer or spiritual meditation purposes.
- Be attentive to the emotional "highs" and "lows" that occur in the group as worship proceeds.
- Keep distractions to a minimum. Be sure that sound systems and videos are ready and working. Keep the tuning of instruments and the worship team movement to a minimum.
- Minimize the number of tempo changes in the songs you choose. If you change the tempo too much, the group will be confused. Either start your worship time with some energetic or upbeat songs, then move toward slower and more meditative time; or start slower and move toward upbeat praise and worship.
- Be humble; be expectant; be responsible; be loving; be yourself!

Understand Your Students!

Every youth worker needs to be a student of the culture. Today's students are different from you and look at the world differently. Here are some things every youth worker needs to know about twenty-first-century students:

They are in a culture that reinvents itself every three to five years. You might feel like you are on the cutting edge with the worship songs and techniques that you highly value. I remember singing a song that I really loved and telling students that it was a contemporary song. One student asked when it was written. When I checked, I found it had been written in 1972! So much for cutting edge. You are going to have to know what's happening in the culture. Listen to students' music. Go to Christian bookstores and ask someone to point out music that most students are listening to. Experiment with drum machines and rhythm tracks on keyboards. Change songs you know into something different by putting the melody with a more aggressive or progressive musical beat. The joy of and frustration with doing ministry with today's students is that you cannot rely on the stuff that has always worked. You've got to know what's happening now! Capitalize on the students' worlds.

They are cross-cultural. Ethnic diversity is not only appreciated; it is embraced. That is going to make a difference in worship experiences. There is no such thing as strictly African-American, Anglo or Hispanic music or worship experiences. The buzzword these days is "multicultural." That's a challenge in worship. Know what's happening with worship around the country. A good leader these days has to have a worldview that embraces all cultures. Subscribe to *Worship Leader* magazine and read books on worship that will broaden your worship horizons.[2]

Technology is a part of students' everyday lives. It is rapidly assimilated. Students are used to computers, power-point presentations, video clips and interactive technology. It has changed their way of thinking and learning. They can take in massive amounts of input. What that means for worship is that you need to find ways to incorporate technology. Ask your students to help you. Remember, when you talk technology, you're talking their language.

Experts tell us that *students learn in six- to eight-minute spurts.* In practical terms, that means you need to keep worship moving and changing. You cannot beat songs to death or do long sets of music without changing something. Capitalize on change to hold students' attention and keep worship experiences fresh. Incorporate different ideas to make transitions in worship interesting.

Students are highly visual learners. Find ways to bathe students' senses. Since we cannot see God, we must find ways to give students visual experiences of the presence of God. Point out in worship experiences when you or a fellow student is being moved or challenged. Stop and give a talk about what is happening. Give students an opportunity to clap their hands. Let them look at something (a video clip, picture, etc.) or give them an opportunity to use their imagination (with a story, imaginary journey, etc.) to add punch to your worship experiences.

We live in a time of high moral relativism. Many students are struggling with the idea of absolute truth. You cannot negotiate on the meaning and power of Christianity. Unashamedly proclaim the name, power and presence of the living God. Remember, Jesus is *the* Way, *the* Truth and *the* Life. Emphasize that to your students over and over again.

Students are serious about life and concerned about their future. Experts affirm that this isn't a carefree generation. Don't be afraid to engage your students in serious worship. Don't apologize for asking them to get into the depths of faith.

Students are highly relational. They need relationships because of the alienation, abandonment and loneliness of their age. Build worship experiences that enhance community. Holding hands, saying prayers in unison and singing together are just a few ways to meet their need and to enhance worship.

You have to be real in worship. Despite what the culture may tell us, image isn't everything. Be willing to be "earthen vessels" (2 Corinthians 4:7, *KJV*). Let them know how you are learning and growing. Let your students see and hear your inner turmoil. Give permission for your students to be real in worship. The last thing we want to do is to encourage them to be stoic in worship.

Use instruments that might be new to your students. Utilize congas or other types of percussion instruments, horns, etc.

Consider themes for each worship team. This would give diversity to each week's worship. For instance, one team would have a ska theme, another R&B or hiphop, etc.

Notes:
1. *Microsoft Bookshelf Dictionary* (Redmond, WA: Microsoft Bookshelf 98, Microsoft Corporation, 1997).
2. See "Suggested Reading" at the end of this book (pp. 115-117).

Tools of Worship

There are not very many true "handymen" in this world. You probably know the type of person I am referring to—someone who knows how to construct, repair, manufacture or craft something of value with his or her bare hands and raw resources. Give a person like that a task, any task, and it is done—and done well!

Without any stretch of the imagination, I know that fixing things is not my calling, or gift. To tell you the truth, if you gave me a pile of raw materials, some hand tools and a few hours to make something, you would return only to find what you left—a pile! Although being a handyman might not be how God designed me, I do know enough about building to know some basic truths that are common knowledge pertaining to every construction task—and to leading worship. Every truth of building can be applied to the act of worship. In fact, when you worship, you *are* building. When you are worshiping, you are doing something that matters in people's lives and in God's heart. You are building an altar or a house of sacrifice and praise unto the Lord.

Building Worship

When you have built worship in a God-honoring manner, guess who shows up? The Lord Himself! The Bible says that God inhabits the praises of His people (see Psalm 22:3, *KJV*). When worship is properly expressed, God moves in. Talk about high take-home value! Read the parable of the house builders in Matthew 7:24-27. To paraphrase the words of Jesus, "Be wise." Build your house of worship on a solid foundation.

Set Excellence as the Goal

Excellence is a worthy goal. We are not talking perfection; rather, we are referring to doing our best. None of us can offer anything to God that is perfect because what we give comes from a corrupt heart. Yet we can bring the best of what we can possibly give as an offering to the One who gave the best of Himself for us! What does that mean in practice?

- *Prepare* the song list. Write out some prayers.

- *Practice* your instruments. Think through the transitions, key changes, etc.

- *Imagine* worship as a gift you are presenting to the Lord.

- *Sing* your heart out.

- *Speak* to the best of your ability.

- *Do* your best.

Practice Patience

Don't expect yourself, your fellow leaders or students to be great at worship all at once. Take time with worship. Worship is not an act that comes naturally to anyone. Even though we were created to worship God, other pursuits in our lives have taken precedence. We are much better at coming to God with all sorts of needs than we are with praises. Celebrate every worship experience that goes well! Learn and grow from those that aren't as successful. Tell your students that you are all growing together. "Wait upon the Lord" (Isaiah 40:31, *KJV*) and God will bless you.

Obtain the Right Tools for the Job

Virtually anything can be a good tool for worship. Prayers, devotional materials, songs, musical instruments, voices, hands and the Bible are tools you would expect to use. But you can also use other tools: a local park, a beach, a hike, a movie, a CD, a picture or a worship leader and/or band from another church. The tool box of a good worship builder is full of creative ideas for how to make worship happen in the lives of your students!

Operate the Tools Skillfully

You need some degree of skill. This cannot be said enough! Leadership requires a certain level of professionalism and competency. You wouldn't put a person who hasn't led a Bible study in front of your students for a key study at a retreat! You would never let someone who has never led a crowd breaker lead one at an event where you have encouraged your students to bring their non-Christian friends. You need to develop some level of skill in leading public prayer, song leading, devotional experiences and other worship tools, for your worship experiences in youth ministry to have the impact you desire.

Develop a Worship Plan

You need to follow a plan. Set spiritual goals for your worship times. Use the worship planning sheets provided in this book (p. 47ff.), or develop one that works for you. Just like a contractor uses a blueprint for construction, have a worship plan that will guide your worship experiences. Put it this way: Would you ever consistently get up to speak to your students without any plan or preparation? No! Put a plan together that will take you step-by-step through a worship time. Not only will it guide your experience, but it will also provide a helpful tool for evaluation afterwards.

Supervise the Process

Ask for feedback from the other leaders and students. Evaluate your worship experiences like you evaluate every other aspect of your ministry. What worked? What didn't? Keep records. Take calculated risks and keep track of how each risk paid off—or didn't. Bring in another worship leader you admire for feedback.

One more comment about supervision—it has to do with spiritual boundaries. This is a sensitive subject, so let me tread carefully; you need to be aware of your church's spiritual boundaries when it comes to worship experiences. Some churches are more demonstrative when it comes to worship and others are more reserved. Talk to your senior pastor about these issues. It would be a shock if your students showed up for worship in the larger context of public worship and started doing things that others considered unacceptable. This is a definite wisdom step for every youth worker. Remember, you are a *servant* of your church. You are not building a church of your own (unless, of course, you are a church planter). Help your students worship in the context of your Christian community with emotional and spiritual integrity.

The Tools

Prayer

Prayer has been the primary tool of good worship for centuries. Much of what we call "worship" is really an expression of communication to God. That, in essence, is what prayer is—communication. Since there are so many ways to come to the Lord in prayer, consider using a number of different styles of prayer in your worship times with students.

SILENT PRAYER

Quiet the room down, play some soft background music (either live or recorded), invite students to close their eyes and come to the Lord in prayer. When we open our lives up to God in prayer, it does not matter what we actually say; we are making our lives and hearts available to the movement of the Holy Spirit.

RESPONSIVE PRAYER

In liturgical churches, you often hear prayers followed by the leader saying, "Lord in Your mercy," and the group responding, "Hear our prayer." Being responsive in this way can further involve your students in prayer. Try having a group prayer. You take the initiative to say, "Lord in Your mercy" after every petition that is shared. Invite the group to respond to you either with a verbal "Amen" or with "Hear our prayer."

GROUP PRAYER

Youth leaders used to call this type of prayer "popcorn prayer." Whatever we call it now, it is an opportunity to open your prayer time up to the group. Have students form small groups. Have them hold hands and pray one at a time. For those students who are intimidated, they can say "Pass." Teach students that God promises that there is real power when Christians agree in prayer.

PRAYER WRITING

One of the best things I have done over the past 10 years in my walk with Jesus has been to write out my prayers. It keeps my prayers focused, it gives me a way to chronicle God's faithfulness and it prevents me from always praying the same thing over and over again. You might want to provide a few minutes, an index card and a pencil to each student during worship. Have them write out a prayer. Collect the index cards. Pray over the pile of cards, then give them out to other students or keep them and put them in a prayer box. Whatever you do, teaching students this habit of prayer will pay off in focused, vibrant prayer lives.

ACTS PRAYER

Adoration, Confession, Thanksgiving, Supplication—ACTS. (There is another variation of this called TRIP—Thanksgiving, Requests, Intercession, Purpose.) Structure your prayer life. You and your students will discover that you will have a more focused and comprehensive prayer life when you use this ACTS method. So often our prayers are reduced to a laundry list of "I want" and "I need" prayers. When we use this simple method, it can help us to pray in a more God-honoring manner that is consistent with what Jesus taught during His ministry. You can also use the ACTS method in public worship settings. Here's one way to do it:

Adoration
- Sing a song of worship.
- Ask the students to take a piece of paper and write down how they feel about the Lord. Tell them that it is okay to write down "I love You, Jesus."

Confession
- Sing another song of worship (or continue with the song above).
- Ask the students to write down the things that they have done in their lives in the last 24 hours that they know didn't please God. Tell them to be specific and to write down at least five words that summarize their confession.
- Continue the singing.

Thanksgiving
- Ask students to write down 10 things in their lives that they are thankful for. They don't have to write long sentences but encourage them to say quietly in their hearts, "God, thank You for...."

Supplication
- Have students write the names of two people they want to pray for. Tell them to be specific about how God could touch the lives of those friends or family members.
- Close with either a song or the students bringing their lists to the worship leader and having the whole group pray silently over the lists as someone in the group shares with the Lord the group members' desire for Him to hear all their prayers together.

INTERCESSIVE PRAYER

Jesus gave us a great model for prayer. In John 17, He prayed with sincerity and intensity for the people He loved. In your worship time, have the students pray for each other. You can do this by simply asking them to form a group and pray for the person on their right/left. Have them draw names for secret prayer partners for a season of time. Have students pair off for prayer during worship times.

Keep a group prayer diary where all prayer requests for people in your group are listed. Be sure to leave room to note answers. Each prayer that God answers can be celebrated. You would be surprised how infrequently we remember what we've prayed for. We need to teach students to praise God for answered prayer.

LAYING ON OF HANDS

The Bible talks frequently about the act of laying on of hands as a form of worship, healing, anointing for ministry and blessing. In a critical world like the one we live in, teaching students to bless others through the laying on of hands would add "high octane" to worship.

Have the students form small groups of five or six. Have one student at a time step into the middle to be prayed for and blessed. Instruct the students to lay hands on the person (on the head, back or shoulder only, please!) and pray for God to bless him or her. When your students are involved in a mission project, encourage leaders and parents to do the same thing as a means of seeking God's power for ministry. Laying on of hands is a powerfully biblical means of prayer that will have a huge impact in your ministry!

GUIDED PRAYER

This type of prayer is helpful as a means of leading students in a prayer time that can be very personal and intimate without requiring them to say a word. Guided prayer is where you, as the leader, pray while the students remain silent. You pray and have periods of silence where you ask students to pray silently according to your guidance or the steps you lay out for them to take. In this instance, you are the prayer tour guide, walking them through a process of prayer for their lives. You do the work—they get the prayer benefit. Here's an abbreviated example of a guided prayer based upon the parable of the Good Samaritan:

- Have the students bow their heads, hold hands and pray silently for several seconds, then continue:

> **Lord Jesus, thank You for the way You have touched our lives.**
>
> **Tonight, we recognized in the Bible that we are not much different from that man who was beaten by the side of the road and left for dead. There have been many ways that we feel all beaten up on the inside. Many of us have those feelings and want so much to give up.**
>
> **Students, tell the Lord right now how you have felt beaten up by life this past week—when have you felt forgotten, ignored, hurt or abused. Tell the Lord silently about it. (Pause.)**
>
> **God, each of us is telling You right now how we have felt so much like that beaten man. We recognize that we don't have a hope in the world except for the fact that You come and rescue us. You pick us up, heal us and put us back on our feet to serve You. And Lord, we praise You for that!**
>
> **Tell the Lord how thankful you are that He is in your life. Let Him know**

how much you praise Him for how He has accepted you and rescued you just the way you are. (Pause.)

After a moment or two of silence, close the prayer.

Readings from the Bible

It should not come as a surprise to you that we can use the Bible as a tool in worship. Since the Bible is the foundation of all we do in ministry, it needs to be put to good use as we lead students to the Lord. Here are some ideas on how to use the Bible in worship:

CHORAL READINGS

Put the Bible passage into a choral or reader's theater format. The following example is adapted from Psalm 150:

Reader 1:	**Praise the Lord.**
Reader 2:	**Praise the Lord.**
Reader 3:	**Praise the Lord.**
All:	**Praise the Lord.**
Reader 3:	**In the church,**
Reader 2:	**In the heavens,**
Reader 1:	**On the street,**
Reader 2, 3:	**In the houses,**
Reader 1, 2:	**In the schools,**
All:	**Wherever people can praise Him,**
Reader 1:	**Praise the Lord.**
All:	**Praise the Lord.**
Reader 1:	**With the sound of a trumpet,**
Reader 2:	**With guitars and drums,**
Reader 3:	**With dancing and singing,**
All:	**With loud cymbals,**
Reader 2:	**With soft voices,**
All:	**With the shout of our hearts, praise the Lord.**
Reader 2, 3:	**Praise the Lord.**
Reader 1, 2:	**Praise the Lord.**
All:	**Praise the Lord!**

RESPONSIVE READINGS

Read Scripture, then lead a response to the passage. For example, after reading Psalm 65, you might use the following response:

Leader: **Lord, it is right for us to praise You.**

Group: **Happy are those whom You have chosen, whom You have brought into Your kingdom to live in You. We shall be happy with the good things You bring and the blessings You shower upon us in Your love.**

Leader: **You answer our needs by giving us victory and You do wonderful things to save us.**

Group: **We all commit our lives to trusting You as Lord, God, Master and Friend.**

DRAMATIC READINGS

Dramatically read a story from the Bible, verbally "acting" out the parts.

INTERSPERSED SCRIPTURE

Underscore your spiritual themes during worship times with strategically placed Bible passages. Memorize them for even more effectiveness.

> **Remember, the Bible is God's Word and it is *alive*! Use it!**

Music

When most youth leaders think worship, they usually think "music." That's good! Music is an expression of the heart. Music gives shape to what is occurring in the spirit of a person. Whether people are singing, playing an instrument, letting a MIDI instrument lead them or using a split-track CD; music can inspire, move, challenge and open us like no other art form when it comes to worship.

Worship music has been around as long as there have been people who have trusted in God. Don't let yourself be fooled—good worship music has been written for centuries. David wrote worship music. Martin Luther wrote worship music. Worship music is being written today.

Be a student of worship music. Personally, I listen to worship music all the time in my car, office and home. Worship music wakes me up on my alarm clock. It not only helps lead my heart to the Lord, but also helps me envision and embody in my own life how worship can take place in ministry.

Listen to various styles of worship music. Choose a worship song and sing it to a different rhythm. This works great, especially if you know how to use drum machines or rhythm tracks on keyboards. You can sing a melody to practically any beat and entirely change the "feel" of the song.

Categorize the types of songs you utilize in worship. Know what songs work best in upbeat praise-oriented moments and what songs work best in quieter moments of reflection. Keep a binder of worship songs that are alphabetized and categorized. Use transparencies of the lyrics.

When choosing songs to sing, use this rule: *If you can't sing them with authenticity, don't lead them.* Always apply songs to your own spiritual life and see if the lyrics prove true. John Fischer, author and a pioneer of contemporary Christian music, advises leaders to choose music that reflects truth. Evaluate each song by answering the following questions:

- Can you sing it with integrity?
- Have you experienced what it is saying?
- Do you believe what it is communicating?
- Is it distorting the faith?
- Is it easy to learn?

Add your own criteria for evaluating worship music.

Use only a certain number of songs during a given period of the year. Let the songs "get under the skin" of the students. Use the songs often enough that the students can sing them without reading the words but not so much that they say "Not that again!" The goal of using music should be to release the worshipers from the printed pages in order to focus more fully on Jesus.

LIST OF SOURCES FOR WORSHIP SONGS

Below is a list of worship-song sources to help you with your planning. You can find most of these resources at your local Christian bookstore. If they are unavailable there, you can contact each publisher individually at the addresses given below.

> **Note:** When you use songs, you are required to have copyright permission. Contact Christian Copyright Licensing International for the most comprehensive clearance available (1-800-234-2446).

- Furious?Records (Sparrow); P.O. Box 5010; Brentwood, TN 37024-59010
- Hillsongs Australia; P.O. Box 1195; Castle Hill NSW 2154 Australia
- Hosanna! Integrity Music; P.O. Box 851622; Mobile, AL 36685-1622
- Maranatha Music; 30230 Rancho Viejo Rd.; San Juan Capistrano, CA 92675
- Mercy Publishing (Vineyard); 5300 E. La Palma Ave.; Anaheim, CA 92807
- Vertical Music by Integrity Incorporated; 1000 Cody Rd.; Mobile, AL 36695

Dance

The Bible puts a big emphasis on a variety of expressions of worship. One of the most joyous—and potentially controversial—is dance. Dance as an expression of worship has a long biblical history. Miriam danced before the Lord after the people of Israel crossed the Red Sea (see Exodus 15:20). David danced before the Lord (see 2 Samuel 6:16). A lame beggar went "walking and jumping, and praising God" after being healed (Acts 3:8). Dance was an integral part of the culture of worship not only in the Jewish faith but also in the Early Church.

It is interesting to me that we use contemporary dances in many ways in youth ministry but not for the sake of worship. Simple line dances can be very effective in a worship atmosphere, especially when singing upbeat songs of celebration and praise. One resource that you might want to capitalize on is Jews for Jesus at (415) 864-2600; ask them to send you a dance representative. The music and teaching ministries of Jews for Jesus have taught many Christians how to dance for joy before the Lord. Hey, why not you?

Other Physical Expressions of Worship

Clapping, shouting, whispering, sitting, jumping, leaping for joy, bowing, prostrating oneself, kneeling, lifting hands, lifting faces to the sky, bowing heads, making banners for worship—there are endless possibilities. Psalm 103:1 says "all that is within me, bless his holy name" *(KJV)*. Let's not confine our worship to just one or two expressions any longer. If a song's lyrics say "lift up our hands," then let's lift our hands. If they say "shout to the Lord," then let's shout. Youth ministry should be the place where we intentionally teach growing believers to open themselves fully in worship before the Lord.

Creative Exercises

You can use just about anything as something that can spark creative worship with your students. Be creative! Some ideas:

- Buy a box of nails at the hardware store and have each student hold a nail while focusing on the sacrifice of Jesus on the cross. After a time of confession, have students hammer the sins they have written on a 3x5-inch index card onto a small cross that you construct out of two-by-fours or fence posts.
- Buy some flash paper.[1] Have each student write his or her biggest failure on a small piece of the paper. Place it in a metal container (e.g., barbeque, trash can), light it and watch it disappear as a demonstration of how God takes our sin and completely wipes it out with His love.

> **Caution:** Please be careful in the use of flash paper. *Never* allow students to use it unsupervised!

- Get a big jar of jelly beans and slowly pour them into a smaller jar. Have the jelly beans overflow onto the table and then fall onto the floor. As the sound of the beans fills the room, talk about the abundant love of Jesus Christ and how His love is overflowing for us.
- Bring a children's book (e.g., *The Runaway Bunny, The Giving Tree, The Velveteen Rabbit, The Chronicles of Narnia*[2]) and read a section that describes the Lord.
- Have the students close their eyes and thank God for a particular attribute in their lives.

- Make a banner.
- Give God regular rounds of applause.
- Have communion together.
- Walk in the rain with your arms uplifted and praise God for His love that washes us "white as snow" (Isaiah 1:18).

Drama

Drama is extremely effective in the context of worship. If the spiritual theme of the worship can be conveyed in a brief drama, you will help students apply that truth to their lives. Drama helps us envision ourselves in life situations. Bringing biblical characters to life through monologues is especially powerful if well prepared. Some easy-to-use drama resources are:

- Willow Creek Community Church in Barrington, Illinois at *www.willowcreek.com*.
- Linneas Publishing Company; P. O. Box 419527; Kansas City, MO 64141
- *Fresh Ideas: Skits and Dramas,* (Gospel Light, 1998). Order direct at 1-800-4-GOSPEL.

The monologue on the following pages was written to depict how the birth of Jesus changed one man's life.

"There's Room in My Heart!"

Costume

A towel wrapped around the actor's head and neck like a turban

Props

Two signs: one marked "No Vacancy" and the other marked "Vacancy"

(Yawning, shuffling around like he just got up, wiping face.) **At last, it's over. What a night! Get this! Get that! Bring me this! I need some help with my luggage over here! People!**

(Looking to heaven.) **Dad, why couldn't you have gotten into a different business than innkeeping? Anything! Sheepherding, cattle ranching, growing grapes and making wine—anything! All those people...**

(In a whining tone.) **"I need an extra towel. I need somebody to clean up after my donkey. I need room service. I need. I need. I need."** *I* **need a gun! Pow!**

Well, finally a little peace now that this blasted Roman census is over. A little vacancy, a little peace!

(Notices the audience.) **Oh, hi! How long have you been here? You don't want a room do ya? I hope not! I might have some vacancies, but I got a secret for ya—the light is on but no one's home, if you know what I mean! Why are you looking at me? Hey, I need a break! The last few nights—wow! Made some extra shekels, but I wonder now if it was all worth it. I'm exhausted.**

Let me tell you what's up: First there's Caesar Augustus. Lousy Romans come in here and start bossing us around. Everybody is on the road: camel jams, nose to tail for miles, and the mess on the sandals—whew!

Then there is the census. Everyone's got to be counted—something to do with taxes.

Next, people everywhere! Not a room left in town. We don't see this very often; Bethlehem is not like Jerusalem. Oh, we have our share of crowds; don't take me wrong. Rabbi Convention every other year; seminars on teaching and circumcision (ouch!). Then there's the Transportation Convention every spring; they bring in all their hyped-up camels and donkeys, newest models. There was this guy trying to pass off a three-humped sports model. What a joke! But this census stuff wasn't like that! Why? Well, at least with the conventions, people *want* **to be here. Not this time!**

Then, in the middle of it all, this couple came to me—baby coming. I felt so sorry for them, but what could I do? "No room in the inn" was all I could say. I told them to check out my buddy Abraham's place down the street, but he was in the same predicament. I saw them standing out in the middle of the street about an hour later—she was in tears and he is about to go ballistic! What could I do? I told them, "Hey, I got a stable out back. It's not the best accommodations, but at least it's cleaner and warmer than the streets."

But then the most amazing thing—later that night I see this light above the place. Shepherds start showing up. I didn't have any more room, but they kept coming. I said, "No room in the inn," and they said, "We're here to see the baby"—something about angels and stuff. I started to get curious about what's happening here! So I asked my kid brother-in-law to watch the front desk and I go to check it out.

I peeked around the door and nearly got blown off my feet. At first I didn't understand, then all of the sudden everything became perfectly clear. I'm not much of a synagogue-goer, if you know what I mean, but this baby was different. Just hearing that baby coo made everything about my life make sense— God, forgiveness, love—gotta tell somebody. There's not room in my inn, but there *is* room in my heart! That seemed to make more sense then than anything else—still does for that matter. How about you? Which sign do you put up in your life? Vacancy or no vacancy?

(Yawning again.) Got to go! The guy in room 201 wants something called "ice"—right!

Meditation Ideas

Meditation has had a bad reputation in Christianity for years. Most people hear the word and immediately bring to mind pictures of hippies, drugs and gurus from the '60s and '70s. Unfortunately, meditation has been used by other religions in ways that are not God-honoring. Meditation for Christians can be a blessing, especially in worship. It gives us an opportunity to reflect, envision and use our imaginations in such a way that our hearts and spirits are engaged. I use Bible stories and exercises that give students an opportunity to get closer to Jesus. Here are two examples:

JESUS ON THE BEACH

Ask students to close their eyes while you read the following:

> **Imagine you are walking along your favorite beach. No one else is there. You are all alone. Feel the spray of the waves against your face. Imagine how you would feel as the water splashes up on your legs as you walk through the surf.** Extend this part out as long as you can to give the students an opportunity to experience the sensations in their imaginations.
>
> **As you are walking along the beach, you notice, way in the distance, another person walking slowly toward you.** Describe various details that take students through a process where the person gets closer and closer to them.
>
> **Imagine the person walking up to you. You notice who it is immediately—it is Jesus! What expression does He have on His face? What is the look in His eyes as He gazes at you? Imagine that, will you? Now, Jesus is going to talk to you. What do you imagine He says? What do you want to say to Him?** Allow students time to pray silently before closing this time of worship.

WORSHIPING THE KING

Read the following illustration:

> **It's Sunday and you're noticing that a huge crowd is gathering near the gate of the city. You've heard some people talk about a man by the name of Jesus and that He claims—as others do—that He is the Son of God. Despite the fact that you have tons of stuff to do as the week is beginning, your curiosity is getting the better of you. You stick around. You decide that you simply want to stand by and watch what's going on. But soon, you are swept up in the crowd. Somebody yells out, "Hey, here He comes." Somebody else asks, "What's He look like?" Another person says, "He's riding a donkey." You strain to take a peek and finally you catch a glimpse of**

Jesus. As you see Him, you notice that other people are laying their jackets down in front of Him; some are yelling, "Praise God"; others are saying "Blessed is the Son of David." What are you feeling? Take a look at Jesus—what does He look like? As He looks around the crowd, what do you notice? What is the expression on His face? If everyone else is praising God, what do *you* want to do? Imagine yourself in the crowd on Palm Sunday; see the sights, feel the emotions, smell the smells, hear the sounds.

PALMS UP, PALMS DOWN

Richard Foster talks about another form of meditation in his book, *The Celebration of Discipline.*[3] It's called a "palms up, palms down" prayer. Begin by having the students put their palms facing down on their laps. Tell them that this symbolizes a desire to turn over any concerns that they may have to God. In the quiet of their hearts, they can be praying something like this: "Lord, I give You my anger toward my dad (mom, sister, brother, friend, etc.). I release my fear of what's going to happen at school today." Whatever it is that weighs on a student's mind can be a "palms down." situation. Now have the students turn their palms up. This is a symbol of their openness to receive from the Lord. For example, "Lord, I would like to receive Your patience and peace today." Whatever students believe they need can be expressed in a "palms up." It works—try it!

SILENCE

Noise surrounds our lives. I remember the first time I took a trip to a Roman Catholic monastery for a few days. The silence of the place nearly wiped me out. Yet, after a few days, I found myself yearning for it and enjoying it because it heightened my awareness of my life before God.

Silence can be a powerful tool in worship. Ask students to close their eyes and be quiet; use the silence to think about a passage of the Bible, to reflect on the message for the night, to envision Jesus speaking to them in some personal way. These moments of silence can be spectacular for your worship times.

MEDIA

Educators are telling us these days that more and more people are sensory learners. What we do know is that much of what we hear is quickly forgotten; but combine our audio stimulus with visual images, and the learning curve goes higher and higher. Media is a great way to worship. Pictures, videos and slides coupled with music and readings can make a great worship experience.

Recently I attended a presentation that had a series of nature pictures, one after another, with music playing in the background. Every 30 seconds or so, a leader from the group would read a portion of a psalm (praise and worship psalms such as Psalms 149 and 150) on the sound system. I found the experience exhilarating. You would be

surprised to find out how many of your students are amateur photographers and musicians, as well as skilled with multimedia programs on the computer. If you're saying to yourself, *I could never do this*, then let your students have a shot at it. Some of the top Christian media companies in the country started with high school students who were given the chance to put together media presentations when they were in high school youth groups.

Atmosphere and Setting

The setting of your worship experience can make it or break it. Before you say, "Well, we don't have a youth room "or "Our pastor doesn't let us use the sanctuary" or "If we were closer to some natural setting like a beach or a park, worship would be easier"—stop! Put one truth in your head and never forget it: You can worship *anywhere*. However, you do need to know what impact the atmosphere that you choose will have on worship time with students. Here are some things for you to consider:

- *Is the room welcoming?* Is it comfortable? Walk around the meeting room and ask if you could see yourself worshiping in that setting.

- *Does the room help students to relax and be themselves?* Worshiping on those hard metal church chairs is a tough job. You might want to have students sit on the floor or wrestling mats. Get some pads or carpet; sometimes having students lie on their backs might be great for worship times.

- *Does the room help students get close to other students?* You don't want them to feel separated from each other. Worship is a community-building event. Get students as close to each other as possible. Place your adult leaders strategically among the students as a way of encouraging participation.

- *What kind of lighting does the room have?* At our church, we have a "disco ball" and a spotlight that we use for worship. It gives that outdoor, starlit look to any room. Over a period of time, when the "stars come out," the students know it is time to worship. Have the lights on dimmer switches, if possible, in order to lower them when necessary. Softer lighting is easier with table or floor lamps versus ceiling fluorescents.

- *What distractions can come into the room?* Are people likely to barge into your room during a worship time? Is it too cold or too hot in the room? Does the sound system you are using buzz or have static during worship? Think through the potential distractions during your worship times and address each as best you can.

- *Is your meeting place constantly exposed to praise and worship?* Worship by yourself or with your team in the room without students. Play worship music in the room as students arrive and leave. Pray that God blesses that space with His presence.

Remember, the purpose is to build a special place of worship with students. I can recall a time when a student told me how much she loved our church's fellowship hall. It wasn't anything special, just a big room. But she remarked, "It's the place where I met the Lord." Places of worship can be powerful in our spiritual lives. Use them to the Lord's advantage.

Other Worship Settings

Some of the most compelling and life-changing worship experiences are ones that do not take place in your usual ministry setting. Be creative in choosing places for worship.

The essence of a setting is creativity and seeing the worship potential in every space. Here is a list of potential settings and corresponding spiritual themes that can be used to enhance worship:

- The desert—wilderness experiences of Jesus or the people of Israel; temptation.
- The ocean or a lake—Jesus walking on water; Jesus calming the storm; Jesus preaching from the edge of Galilee.
- A forest or a mountain trail—the Sermon on the Mount; the Parable of the Sower; wilderness wanderings of the Old Testament.
- The middle of a field where a crop of vegetables is growing—what it means to grow in the Lord; being fruitful versus unfruitful; fruit of the Holy Spirit in Galatians 5.
- An inner-city church or a congregation of another denomination—the diversity and miracle of the body of Christ.
- A park while it's raining—the forgiveness of Jesus; the power of baptism; how God cares for us.
- Make a small prayer closet, room or chapel for small-group or individual worship experiences. This could be a closet or small storage room at the church (or even a church bus or van) that has a small lamp, an open Bible and a small tape player for playing worship music. When I was a camp director in Northern California, there was a hollowed-out tree that was our staff's secret worship center. Often four or five staff members would be MIW (Missing In Worship)!

Notes:
1. Flash paper is highly flammable paper that disappears the instant it is lit with a match or lighter. It makes a spectacular flash when ignited. Flash paper is available in magician supply shops around the country. Another source is the One Way Street Puppet Company in Englewood, Colorado. Their web site is www.onewaystreet.com, or you can reach them by phone at 1-800-569-4537. Please be careful in the use of this paper. NEVER allow students to use it unsupervised.
2. One suggested selection from *The Chronicles of Narnia* comes from the book *The Horse and His Boy*, (New York: Collier Books, 1954), pp. 155-159. This passage tells of a powerful healing conversation between the main character, Shasta, and Aslan. There are many sections in these seven C. S. Lewis books that bring to life aspects of God that are worship worthy.
3. Richard Foster, *The Celebration of Discipline* (San Francisco: Harper and Row, 1988), pp. 30, 31.

Worship Ideas

Activities

On Your Knees

Our physical posture has a powerful impact on our worship lives. Sing some songs of worship to the Lord and, instead of having students stand or sit, ask them to get on their knees for the worship time. Tell them about the importance of humility before God. Read a couple of passages about praying before the Lord on our knees (see Psalm 95:6; Philippians 2:10). In the history of the faith, this type of worship has literally changed lives. Give it a try!

Giving to the Lord

Have students read Matthew 2:1-12. It is the familiar story of the Magi's visit to the baby Jesus after His birth. Teach a Bible study on the passage. Talk about how each of the gifts that were presented to Jesus were not only gifts of worship, but each also symbolized something important. Gold was a gift of honor to a King who would rule by love. Frankincense was a gift for a priest to be used in sacrifices and showed that Jesus would be our sacrifice for salvation. Myrrh was used in burials and foretold the death and resurrection of Jesus.

After explaining the gifts, ask students: **What gift can you present to the King of kings?** You might even want to ask them to prepare a gift to bring prior to the worship time so that it can be well thought out. Maybe they could come up with a gift that would symbolize something that they need to bring to Jesus—for example, a page of a journal to demonstrate their willingness to share with the Lord their deepest thoughts or a dirty sock that symbolizes their need for cleansing. Allow students to be creative in worship when you give to the Lord.

Dark Room

This is a simple idea that is very effective. Find the darkest room in your church campus. Have the group gather in the room for worship. Sing songs, then pray. Turn out the lights so that it is pitch dark. Talk about the darkness of our lives and the world. Instruct students to think how life would be if we lived in darkness all the time. Read and memorize 1 John 1:5: "This is the message we have heard from him and declare to you: God is light; in him there is no darkness at all." Tell students that Jesus is the light of the world and that in Him "there is no darkness." Sing a song about Jesus being the light of the world ("Shine, Jesus, Shine," for example) while you light a single candle. Point out how something so small can make a huge impact. Encourage them to make commitments to shine the light of their faith, reminding them that even small lights can make a big difference in the lives of their families and friends. Quietly sing songs of commitment with the light of the single candle shining.

Make It Personal

Take a prayer or psalm from the Bible or a prayer or hymn from one of your church's prayer or hymn books and personalize it. Anything made more personal is what worship is all about—heart-to-heart encounters with the Lord. Here are some examples:

- The Lord's Prayer: "My Father, You are in heaven and how I worship Your holy name"—for every "us," insert a "my" or a person's name.
- A confession from a hymnal: "Almighty God, before You my heart is open, my desires known, and from You, none of my secrets are hid."
- From a hymnal: "God, I want to count my blessings. One by one, I want to name them before You." (Allow a moment for silence as students recount the blessings of God in their lives.) "As I count my blessings, I realize that they are from You and You alone. I also praise You that You have done great things in my life."
- Psalm 115:1: "Not to me, Lord, not to me but to Your name I give glory because of your loving kindness and because of Your truth."

Drop the Lord a Note

Hand out envelopes and notepaper at the beginning of worship. Have students address the envelopes to God. Instruct each student to write a simple letter to God during the worship time and place it in an envelope, addressing it to him- or herself and seal it. Have them turn in the letters to you for you to keep. About three to six months later, hand the unopened letters back to the students. Spend some time in prayer about the letters. Then ask: **How many of the prayers in your letters were answered? Are your concerns the same today as they were months ago? What has God done in your lives since then?**

Passing God's Peace

In some denominational circles, "passing the peace" is a regular part of a Sunday worship service. Consider using the same thing on a regular basis. Here's how it works: Engage students in a confessional prayer. Have them focus on areas of their lives for which they need forgiveness. Ask each member of the group to hug or shake hands with as many people as possible and say to each of them, "The Lord forgives you." This makes forgiveness personal as well as providing group affirmation.

Look at Your Life on a Deeper Level

Start your devotional time by explaining: **Jesus calls us to a deeper examination of our lives every day. Even so, much of the time we live an unexamined life. The Lord calls us to learn from Him how to be humble and trusting. There are three levels of humility that I want you to pray about specifically for your life.** Give students time to pray silently between each explanation.

- **First level of humility—What are the areas of your life where you are being rebellious against the lordship of Jesus? What areas would God want you to change if you would let Him? Pray about that now.**
- **Second level of humility—What are things that you do in your life where you try to gain all the attention for yourself? When you do something for the Lord, how do you take the credit instead of letting Jesus be praised?**
- **Third level of humility—How are you holding back parts of your life from being controlled by the Spirit of God? If the Lord were to ask you to do something heroic for *Him*, would you trust Him enough to do it?**

   Think for a moment—who are the people in your life who have demonstrated each level of humility? Who are your Christian heroes? Spend a moment in prayer thanking and praising God for these wonderful people of faith!

Prayer or Bible Raps

Put on a drum machine with a hip-hop beat and recite Bible passages together with the whole group. This works great for Scripture memorization. One of my favorites is Romans 8:28. We came up with a simple rap:

   In all things...in all things...in all things...God works for...the good of those who love Him...ugh!

Have students dance and clap their hands. Make the volume loud and get them really worshiping with joy and celebration.

Melodrama Readings

Take stories or sections from the Bible that talk about opposites and turn the reading into a melodrama. Have the students cheer and boo. Here are a couple of Bible texts that work well:

   Galatians 5:16: But I say, walk in the Spirit (yeah!) And you will not carry out the desire of the flesh (boo!). For the flesh (boo!) sets its desire against the Spirit (boo!) and the Spirit against the flesh (yeah!) *(NASB)*.

Philippians 4:4-7: Rejoice in the Lord (yeah!) always; (yeah!) again I will say rejoice (yeah!)! Let your forbearing spirit be known to all men. The Lord is near (yeah!). Be anxious (boo!) for nothing, but in everything by prayer and supplication with thanksgiving (thank you Lord!) let your requests be made known to God (hear, Lord!). And the peace of God, (yeah!) which surpasses all comprehension, (yeah!) shall guard your hearts and your minds in Christ Jesus (yeah!) *(NASB)*.

Prayers and Devotionals

Stealth Prayer

You've heard of stealth bombers—those aircraft that can't even be detected by radar. How about challenging students to be "stealth pray-ers." Wherever you go as a youth group, tell your students to silently pray for everyone they see. We call these "prayers of bombardment." As you're walking around a mall, pray for each person you see on the escalator. A simple prayer that God would touch them is all we're expecting in this instance. At an amusement park, instead of simply meeting for lunch, meet for short prayer times for the people students run into during the day. Make every experience a prayer/worship experience.

Play-Dough Prayer

Buy play dough. Give each student a small container of the dough. Read Jeremiah 18 which talks specifically about being clay in our Lord's hands. Have students kneed the dough with their eyes closed. Ask questions for their reflection, such as: **How is the Lord trying to fashion you?** Tell them to form a rough edge, then ask: **What rough edges do you have in your life?** Invite the students to smooth out the edges, then ask: **What would the Lord have to do to have the rough edges of your life smoothed out?** Close by leading students in silent prayer.

Power Praying

So much of the time, we pray for the needs people share with us or the concerns that are obvious in a person's life. Open new prayer possibilities by explaining that God wants to do more than meet the needs we can see. Take a lesson from Paul in the New Testament. In Ephesians 1:18,19, Paul prays for the people of Ephesus: "I pray also that the eyes of your heart may be enlightened in order that you may know the hope to which he has called you, the riches of his glorious inheritance in the saints, and his incomparably great power for us who believe." He knew these people well and could have spent time simply praying for the things of which he was aware. But he went deeper and prayed for big stuff like enlightenment, hope and power. How about praying for these things for each other in your group? Take a section of Scripture and pray that the truth or character trait that is specified in the section be actualized in the students' lives. That's more than just "I want" prayers—that's power praying.

Prayer Lights

Buy a box of four- to five-inch candles—the kind that many churches use on Christmas Eve. Make a place in the meeting room where you can put several lit candles—a makeshift altar, a piece of plywood on the floor or something similar. (**Remember:** A youth leader must always be safety conscious. Place a metal pan or cookie sheet on the altar or board; and no matter where you have lit candles, make sure that you have the means to extinguish the flames in case of an emergency.)

Have students read the Great Commission in Matthew 28:18-20 together:

> Then Jesus came to them and said, "All authority in heaven and on earth has been given to me. Therefore go and make disciples of all nations, baptizing them in the name of the Father and of the Son and of the Holy Spirit, and teaching them to obey everything I have commanded you. And surely I am with you always, to the very end of the age."

Read Matthew 5:13-16:

> You are the salt of the earth. But if the salt loses its saltiness, how can it be made salty again? It is no longer good for anything, except to be thrown out and trampled by men. You are the light of the world. A city on a hill cannot be hidden. Neither do people light a lamp and put it under a bowl. Instead they put it on its stand, and it gives light to everyone in the house. In the same way, let your light shine before men, that they may see your good deeds and praise your Father in heaven.

After the reading, talk about believers as lights to the world and have each student light a candle for five people with whom they can share their faith. Have them put the candles, when lit, on the board or makeshift altar. See how the lights grow stronger and stronger. Each represents a prayer before God for salvation.

"You Are Loved" Prayer

Buy small mirrors at a cosmetic store or discount store, one for each student. Lead a time of song worshiping the Lord for His love. Sing the first verse of "Amazing Grace." Ask God to bless each student with a strong sense of the love God has specifically for each of them. Instruct students to look into their own mirrors and say quietly to themselves, "You are loved. Jesus died for you. You are loved with an incomparable love."

Write a Poem Prayer

It's amazing to me how students love poetry. Have each student write a poem to God. Play music in the background. Reassure students that no one is going to evaluate their poems; this is simply a way to write something special from their hearts to God's heart.

Prayer Post-Its

Have the students write out their prayer requests for themselves, others or major concerns in their lives on self-stick notes. Have them place the notes on a cross that you make, on a special bulletin board you set aside or even on the ceiling of the room you normally meet in. Let the notes grow in number over a few weeks; then remove them and see how many prayers God has answered. Read every answered prayer. For every answer, have the group say or even yell out, "Yea, God!" Remember, the Bible tells us that we should shout our praises to God (see Psalm 47:1; 66;1; 95:1).

Laser and Spotlight Prayer

Almost every church has a spotlight and a laser pointer these days. If not, buy a cheap spotlight at a local hardware store. You can also pick up a laser pointer from an office supply store. Use these to talk about how God sees into our lives. Turn out the lights and shine the spotlight around the room. Some of the students will cover their eyes because the light is so bright. Explain: **That is how God sees our lives. He bathes our lives with His light. If we live in His light, there won't be any darkness. "This is the message we have heard from him and declare to you: God is light; in him there is no darkness at all. If we claim to have fellowship with him yet walk in the darkness, we lie and do not live by the truth. But if we walk in the light, as he is in the light, we have fellowship with one another, and the blood of Jesus, his Son, purifies us from all sin" (1 John 1:5-7).**

   Pray about the dark areas of your own life and your students' lives. Then take the laser pointer and flash it on students' hearts. Continue: **We would never use a laser pointer to see an entire person, but we would use one to shine on something very specific—that's the way the Lord looks at us. Sometimes, He shines His whole light on our lives; sometimes He needs to focus on something specific so that He can reveal it and heal it. Is there a deep secret that God wants to shine the light of His love on in your life?** Instruct students to be specific in their prayer time with God.

Sign-Language Prayer

Students have been exposed to sign language in school and on television. Have a student who knows how to sign prepare some of your group's favorite songs or prayers and teach the rest of the group how to sign the songs or prayers. It will make the worship much more personal, visible and fun!

Prayer for Healing

God is interested in healing the whole person. So much of the time we restrict healing prayer to just what we see in a person's body. God wants to do so much more! How about praying for the healing of emotions, spirits, relationships and bodies? Pass out adhesive bandages at the beginning of the worship time. At a designated time, have students place the bandage on some part of their bodies that represents where they need prayer. For example, if they put it on their forehead, it could mean to them that they have a headache or that they are dealing with some thoughts that are not God-honoring. Have students form small groups and pray for those hurts. Read James 5:13-15, then instruct them about the practice of laying on of hands (see Acts 9:17-19; 28:8,9).

Prayer Cards

Using a 3x5-inch index card, design a prayer card for each student prior to the meeting, preprinted with one of the following statements on it: "This is my most pressing need today" or "This is an area of my life where I am really struggling." During worship time, have everyone write a prayer request on his or her card, but not sign the card. Collect all the cards and redistribute them to the group members. After the cards are redistributed, spend some time in silent prayer. Have each student pray for the person whose prayer-request card they now have. The requests are anonymous so it isn't threatening, yet it is personal and it can be life-changing.

Thanks to the Lord

Read Luke 17:11-19. Jesus heals ten lepers and only one returns to thank Him. This is a great story about thankfulness before God. How often this story parallels our lives. We are so busy asking Jesus for what we need that we forget to come back to the Lord in worship for answered prayer. This is not only a story that can be a launching pad for you to teach on the subject of prayer, but it can also become a worship experience. Read the story aloud to the students. Sing songs of thankfulness to God. Ask students to think about any blessing that they have recently received for which they have forgotten to thank God. Have them write a prayer of thanksgiving and praise. During the worship time, read a couple of prayers to the group as a means of adoration to God. Then form a circle and have students share things they are thankful for in their lives in group prayer. We need to intentionally build thankful hearts in the lives of students.

Stations of the Cross or The Seven Last Words of Christ

For these ideas, you'll need to purchase some art slides or a video on the life of Jesus. There are "Stations of the Cross" slides available through Harbinger Communications (800-320-7206.) There are also many different videos on the life of Jesus available in video stores or from Christian publishing houses. Show slides or a video on the death of Jesus. Pause during dramatic moments in the presentation. Ask students to meditate or think about the sacrifice of Jesus. Pause at the end of each "station." Ask students to reflect on their feelings at that moment in the suffering of Jesus.

For the "The Seven Last Words," ask students to pray concerning:

"FATHER, FORGIVE THEM" (LUKE 23:34)
Theme: We need to be forgiven and to forgive.
Question: In what areas of our lives do we need forgiveness? Who do we need to offer what Jesus so freely offers to us?

"TODAY, YOU WILL BE WITH ME IN PARADISE" (LUKE 23:43)
Theme: Our desire is to hear those words from Jesus.
Questions: How much do you long to be in the presence of Jesus? How much do you depend on the Lord when you are going through tough times?

"HERE IS YOUR MOTHER" (JOHN 19:27)
Theme: Jesus reinforced our need for relationships.
Questions: What relationships do you depend on during crises? Thank God for those relationships now.

"MY GOD, MY GOD, WHY HAVE YOU FORSAKEN ME?" (MATTHEW 27:46)
Theme: We sometimes feeling abandoned by God.
Questions: Have you ever felt separated from God? What did you do about it? How did God reach out to you?

"I AM THIRSTY" (JOHN 19:28)
Theme: Jesus needed some refreshment for His dying body.
Questions: Where do you turn when you need to feel better? What gets you down? How does God refresh you?

"IT IS FINISHED" (JOHN 19:30) AND "FATHER, INTO YOUR HANDS I COMMIT MY SPIRIT" (LUKE 23:46)
Theme: Jesus completed the purpose of His death for our salvation.
Questions: What are the first words you would love to hear from Jesus when you enter His presence? What is the mission you are to accomplish with your life in the Lord Jesus?

Worship Planning Sheets

In preparation for worship experiences in your youth ministry, use the following guidelines to provide the information you will need to carry out your plan. Samples of completed planning sheets and blank sheets follow the explanations.

Remember, these are just suggested forms. Use them to develop planning sheets that work for you!

How to Use the Worship Planning Sheets

Specific Ministry

Describe the ministry that you are leading in worship—junior high, high school, college.

Context of the Meeting

Every worship experience should take into account the context of the meeting. These factors will help you determine the scope and depth of the worship you plan. Is it for a weekend retreat, camp, backpack trip, Bible study, worship night, leaders' meeting, outreach or community event?

Spiritual Level of Students

Without being judgmental, ascertain where students are spiritually. Are they relatively unchurched, as they would be in an outreach event? Are they relatively new in the Lord? Are many of them long-term believers? What is their previous worship experience? These factors will be important in planning a worship event that will take students to the next step in their walk with God.

Objectives

What do you want to accomplish in the worship experience? What is your goal? Is the worship time for celebration? Deeper spiritual reflection? Growth? Challenge? Preparation for a specific message? Be specific.

Spiritual Theme

Choose a specific theme and plan accordingly. For example, the theme might be God's faithfulness, God's availability through prayer, God's power to move in our lives, humility, brokenness, etc. A definite theme will add cohesiveness to the worship experience.

My Prayer for the Students

Remember, we don't change lives, God does. Even if you put together a brilliant worship experience, God is the One who is the instigator of all that happens. He created worship and is the focal point of it. Even so, be bold in writing out a prayer of what you expect to happen.

Worship Preparation Sheet

What Is Needed?

- Materials/Tools
- Resources
- Setting/Setup
- Who will be responsible for each part

List everything you will need to carry out the worship. What tools are you going to use? Will you need an overhead projector, guitars, song sheets, rehearsals, lighting, Bibles, transportation, etc.? Who will be responsible for obtaining materials, setting up equipment, etc.? Be specific.

Strategy

Get specific. How are you going to accomplish your worship objective? What creative ideas do you need to brainstorm with your team?

Songs

Have songs ready. Don't ad-lib! Be sure that the selections complement the theme. Whether you use a praise band, a single instrument or CDs, have the songs prepared ahead of time. Also have overhead transparencies, song sheets or other materials prepared. Pay special attention to the following:

- **Order**: Prepare a specific order for the worship songs. Decide if you will begin with a lively active mood; then move into a quiet, reflective mood or vice versa. Will the songs be interspersed with other elements such as prayer, confession or Scripture reading? Will you introduce a new song?
- **Leaders**: Choose a leader who is prepared to lead. Have a rehearsal. Be sure that leaders know the order and are familiar with the songs.

Bible Passages

Have the passages chosen ahead of time to aid the smooth flow of worship. Consider memorizing key transitional passages.

- **Order**: Just as for the songs, prepare the order. Decide where Scripture passages will be used in the order of the worship experience. If they will be interspersed with the songs or other worship elements, be sure that the leaders and readers are aware of the order.

- **Readers**: Decide who will read the Scripture. If students will be reading, be sure they know where they are in the order of worship so you aren't hunting for someone who decided to go to the bathroom. If possible, give the readers the passages a day or two ahead of time to practice reading, or even memorize the passages. Help them with the pronunciation of difficult words. Be sure they have at least a basic understanding of what they are reading.

Creative Experiences

Assemble the worship team and ask, "What can we do to enable God to bless our worship time?" Pray together. Brainstorm; think outside the lines. Glean some ideas from this book. Use drama, readings, written prayers, the ACTS prayer method, biblical meditation exercises, walks, silence, etc.

Decide who will lead specific activities. Remember, leaders lead and people will follow! Lead people to God!

Worship Evaluation Sheet

Evaluation will help you grow as a leader. It will also help with future planning for more effectiveness and fruitfulness. Evaluate with your leadership team and/or have trusted students help. Don't take the comments personally. Remember, your purpose in evaluating is to make worship more effective, not to shoot the messengers. Discuss the following:

- What Worked
- What Did Not Work
- What We Can Learn from the Experience
- Other Comments or Ideas for Future Experiences

Reminder: Attach all readings, written prayers or any other materials to the evaluation sheet for future reference.

Worship Plan Sheet

(Taken from an actual worship experience planned for our youth ministry.)

Meeting Date

October 6

Specific Ministry

Junior High—seventh and eighth graders—FOCUS (Followers Of Christ Undoubtedly Saved) Ministry

Context of Meeting

Regular Wednesday night meeting to kick off our new FOCUS teaching year. We will be gathering together with our returning eighth graders and our new seventh grade students. Many of the seventh graders have been very involved in children's ministry and in the children's music and worship ministry in the past and have a growing sense of worship. The eighth graders still need some work. The worship experience will be the opening 15 minutes of the evening prior to dinner and Bible study.

Spiritual Level of Students

Mixed: We have at least a dozen kids who are here because their parents forced them to come. Two-thirds of the group are growing Christians with a lot of enthusiasm for the Lord. The remaining one-third are either new to the Lord or to our church's ministry.

Objectives

- To introduce the group to worship;
- To show students that we can have fun praising God;
- To demonstrate how we will begin each week during our ministry with a specific God-focus.

Spiritual Theme

The importance of worshiping the Lord: God commands it and has created us to praise Him. No matter what our relationship with Him might be, God calls us to give ourselves to the Lord in a lifestyle of worship.

My Prayer for the Students

Lord God, this is an important year in the life of these students. I am so excited about the opportunity to be their spiritual leader and friend in You. God, I worship You for giving me the time, gift and passion to minister to these students and to participate in what You are doing in their lives. I pray that You will cause a deep hunger for Your presence to come into the life of each student. Through this simple experience, may they see You, know You and grow to love You more. Would You give us the honor of using our team to usher these students into Your presence tonight? I love You, Lord.

Worship Preparation Sheet

What Is Needed?

Memorize the scripture for the evening.

MATERIALS/TOOLS

Song list copied for all the musicians.
Overhead transparencies ready.
Home videotape of trees, ocean, etc. depicting creation.
Have the big screen television ready for video use.

SETTING/SETUP

Worship team rehearsal at 5:30 P.M.
Tuning of instruments at 5:45 P.M.
Have a leadership prayer time before we begin—in front of the students as they are gathering.

WHO WILL BE RESPONSIBLE

Ask someone in the group to change the overheads when needed.

Strategy

SONGS
- **Order**
  "I Love Your Grace," Rick Founds, Maranatha Music
  "Everything I Am," Rory Moland, Maranatha Music
  "Mighty Savior," Danny Daniels, Mercy Publishing
  "Radical God," Kurt Johnson. Mr. J Publishing
  "Shout to the Lord," Darlene Zschech, Hillsongs Music
- **Leaders**
  Jeff (leader), Robin, B. J., Aaron (on bass), Howie, Michelle, Jenna

BIBLE PASSAGES
- **Order**
  Psalm 22:3: We were created to praise God.
  Revelation 5: We will be praising God for eternity.
- **Readers**
  Robin

CREATIVE EXPERIENCES

- After the first three songs, dim the lights.
- Play the videotape depicting creation.
- As the students are watching the video, lower the volume and ask them to close their eyes. Ask for quiet as they are challenged to consider: "What is the first thing about God that crosses your mind when you see the beauty of creation? What is one thing you can say to God about how He put together the world?"
- After there is a moment of silence, lead students in singing "Radical God."
- After the first verse, interrupt and say something such as, "Do you know that you were wired by God to praise Him and to thank Him for who He is and what He has brought into your life? You and I weren't made just to enjoy what God has made but to enjoy God Himself. That's what we call worship, and we're going to be doing it not only here on earth but for an eternity. Pray silently, thanking God for who He is right now."
- End the time with the students standing and singing "Shout to the Lord."

Worship Evaluation Sheet

What Worked

- Students enjoyed the video.
- The songs were well received and singing was enthusiastic.

What Did Not Work

1. The students were a bit rowdy when worship time started.
2. There were a few behavior problems.

What We Can Learn from the Experience

1. **Rowdiness:** Maybe we could have a brief announcement period or even a game early in the meeting to get some energy out of the students in preparation for the worship time.
2. **Behavior problems:** We need to have our adult leaders interspersed throughout the group to give leadership and behavioral accountability to the group members.

Other Comments or Ideas for Future Experiences

There is a huge potential for worship this year. The first-year group is poised for some good stuff! Let's go for it!

Reminder: Attach copies of materials used.

Worship Planning Sheet

Meeting Date

Specific Ministry

Context of Meeting

Spiritual Level of Students

Objectives

Worship
Planning
Sheets

Spiritual Theme

My Prayer for the Students

Worship Preparation Sheet

What Is Needed?

MATERIALS/TOOLS

SETTING/SETUP

WHO WILL BE RESPONSIBLE

Strategy

SONGS

- **Order**

- **Leaders**

BIBLE PASSAGES

- **Order**

- **Readers**

CREATIVE EXPERIENCES

Worship Evaluation Sheet

What Worked

What Did Not Work

What We Can Learn from the Experience

Other Comments or Ideas for Future Experiences

Reminder: Attach copies of materials used.

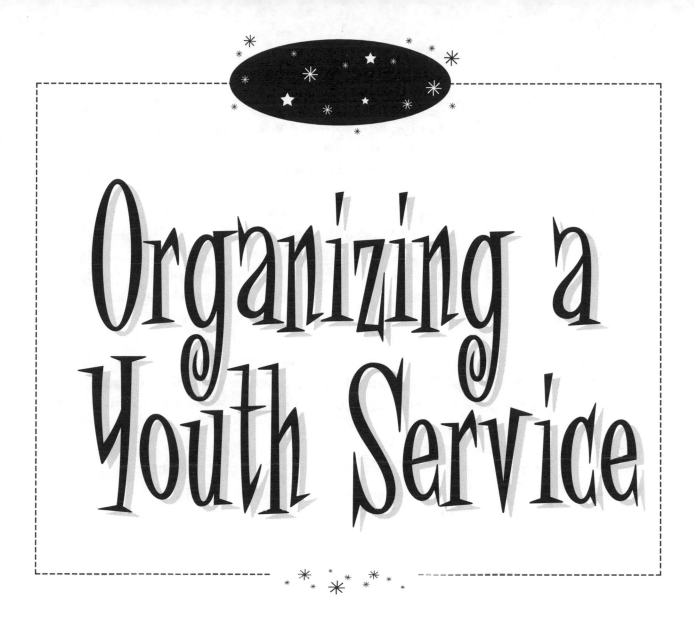

Organizing a Youth Service

Help! I Need to Put Together a Youth Service for Church

What Makes a Good Youth Service?

The purpose of a youth worship service should be just that—worship, not a youth performance. When the pastor asks you to prepare a youth service for the whole church, it's an opportunity for the congregation to meet the youth and for the youth to participate in church. That is a good thing! The service that students lead should be put together with love, integrity and goals that enable students to demonstrate to the larger body their growing faith and enthusiasm for Christ. Design a service that gives the church a taste of what happens when students worship in youth ministry meetings, but do it in such a way that it invites the congregation to worship as well. If you blend the two, you'll have a win-win situation in the long run. These services are great for developing support and encouragement for the youth ministry.

Give permission for the students to be themselves. Don't expect students to be anything more than what they are—high school or junior high students. They are not great preachers (yet!), nor are they seasoned worship leaders. I suggest that you lead side by side with them. It gives the church an opportunity to see how you interact with the students. You could talk for years about your relationships with the youth of your church and it won't equal what adults can see for themselves in a few minutes. Be supportive when a student blows a reading—be patient when your youth band messes up a chord transition. Remember, the point isn't perfection but exposure and experience in leading worship.

Amazingly, the congregation will let students get away with quite a bit in a setting like this—of course, they are "just kids" in many of the adults' minds. So you can push the envelope if you feel led to. Challenge the congregation musically and spiritually. Seize the moment!

Use interviews and testimonies of the students. Here's a suggestion: You preach the sermon and use testimonies from students or an interview of a student or two to make illustrations come to life. If you plan to let a student or two preach, give them a rough idea about how to put together a Bible message. Tell them to:

- Select a Bible passage that means something to them;
- Write out why it is important;
- Think of a life experience that meant something to them and how it relates to the passage.

Prepare some challenges or applications to other people's lives. Rehearse the sermon with them beforehand. Go over the students' work. Give them illustration or story suggestions. If you help them succeed, it will help you succeed!

Get permission for the student worship team or band to lead the worship. Have as many students on the platform as possible. Put microphones up to pick up their voices. There will be many students who don't want to do anything but sing. Participating in a group helps the shyest of students to participate, so I would suggest that your adult leader be the key leader of the worship songs; but if you have a student you can trust, great! Sometimes students get in a larger setting and freeze or clam up. Pick songs that demonstrate the quality of worship in the youth ministry. Choose songs the students sing well and enjoy. Also, choose a song or two that will stretch the congregation by having them raise hands or clap. (But don't push the congregation *too* much if they are not regularly exposed to this much spiritual enthusiasm!)

If your church is used to having printed orders of service, then follow suit and print out the youth service. Have all the songs printed out or on a screen. Use power point,

slides or overhead projectors if you regularly use these. Remember, the point of worship is participation. Making participation as easy as possible will get the congregation on board with what you are doing!

As you plan the service, have a vision of what you want the service to be. Then match your vision with various elements of worship that will move your plan into reality. For example, if you and your worship team want the service to be one that gives the congregation a taste of how your students regularly worship in youth ministry, then design the service with a variety of creative experiences and musical expressions. If you simply want students to be leading what the congregation would normally do in corporate worship, then be sensitive as you plan to bring in elements of worship that will create that climate. Use your worship tools wisely and strategically. Ask the senior pastor to give not only behind-the-scenes support to your youth service but also a verbal acknowledgment during the service. This will be important not only to the students who are leading but to the congregation as well. Public pastoral validation and support are so important in building a prevailing and growing youth ministry.

Sample Youth Service Worship Experience

Use as many or as few of the following elements for your service as you like. This is just one possible order. Many churches use a much simpler order of service. That's okay. Many other churches are more complex. Included here are many of the elements that could fill out an entire worship experience. You choose what components work for your setting.

Special Note: Have as many students as possible serve as ushers, greeters, nursery attendants, etc. Inundate your church with students. You'll be surprised what a blessing this will be to your church. Many church members believe that youth ministry is too separate from the church already, so this is your opportunity to immerse students in the church body.

Gathering Music

Have the youth band or group sing gathering songs. This is a great opportunity to sing more songs.

Announcements

After the senior pastor introduces the service, take the time to make general church announcements. You might want to be even more creative by having some of your students dramatically present the announcements. You can do this by writing the announcements in a television commercial format that can be presented here.

Caution: Announcements made later in the service might unnecessarily break the flow of the worship experience.

Opening Worship Song

Begin worship with two or three celebration songs of worship and praise.

Opening Prayer

Either have a student pray for the service or use a written, responsive prayer such as the following:

Leader: **Praise the Lord! Let us thank the Lord with all our hearts!**

People :   **How amazing are the deeds of our God. Everyone who delights in the Lord should praise the Lord for His mighty works of love.**

Leader: **Everything God does shows His glory and majesty.**

People: There is no way that we can forget or ignore the wonders of God.

Leader: Coming before our Lord with tenderness and humility demonstrates a heart of worship, so come to the Lord. Open your hearts to Him. He is patient and merciful. He is worthy to be worshiped.

People: Lord, we come to You. Rescue us from our unfaithfulness. Build us up through Your Spirit. Our knees are often weak. Our hearts are often in despair. Lead us to Christ our Rock. Heal and forgive us. Strengthen and lead us to see the love of God grow in and through our lives. Amen.

OR

Leader: We gather together to praise our God who has done marvelous thing and who loves us with an uncomparable love.

People: God's love is growing and He has brought us to this place and made us to be His own.

Leader: Our God is a God of faithfulness and grace. He proclaims, "I am the same yesterday, today and forever. I stand at the door of your life and knock. I want to come to you and share my heart and joy."

People: Countless lives have been changed by the love of God. Praise the Lord that He desires to be here as we worship. Let's acknowledge today that He is the King of kings and Lord of lords.

Leader: In a moment of silence, we come to the Lord to examine our lives and allow His Spirit to minister to our hearts.

People: Lord, we come to You. You know our needs better than we do. You know the secrets of our hearts even when we try to hide from You. Reach down deep within our souls and transform us with Your love. Make our lives something You can use to bring Your love to others. Thank You Jesus.

Leader: This is the good news of Jesus—He forgives, encourages and free us. Isn't that great news? Isn't it true that there is no greater love than the love of Jesus? Let's continue our worship of our loving Lord.

People: Amen.

Singing

Making a transition in worship using slower and more meditative songs enables a congregation to begin focusing not only on the power and presence of God but also on their need for God in their lives. Some suggestions:

- Special songs sung by a young person or a youth choir/ensemble.
- Drama, puppet ministry, media or interview that is put together by the students.

Bible Reading

Read a section or two of the Bible. Either have students read them or put the readings in a responsive or readers' theater format. An example, using John 1:1-5:

Leader: **In the beginning was the Word,**

People: **and the Word was with God, and the Word was God.**

Leader: **He was with God in the beginning.**

People: **Through him all things were made; without him nothing was made that has been made.**

Leader: **In him was life,**

People: **and that life was the light of men.**

Leader: **The light shines in the darkness,**

People: **but the darkness has not understood it.**

Leader: **In the beginning was the Word of God**

People: **and the Word of God is Jesus Christ. He is the God of light, life and our salvation.**

The Sermon

Present the sermon through preaching by the youth leader(s), students, interviews, testimonies or dramatic presentations.[1]

Worship Song or Songs

Led by students or the student band.

Monologue

Present a monologue that gives you an opportunity to dramatically show how lives are changed by a relationship with Jesus. A student could write one, you could write one or use one similar to the following:

Thomas—Today

Tom enters sanctuary; sits on stool located center stage.

Hi, my name is Tom. I don't necessarily know why I'm here today to talk to you, but it just seems to be the right thing to do. Maybe I can tell you some things I have learned and how I learned them. Maybe everything will make sense to you. I don't know how to make sense of all of it myself, but I do know one thing— what happened to me changed my life.

This is it—you see, I've always been kind of a suspicious person. Call me a pragmatist, a materialist, a skeptic—whatever you want to call me. "I've got to

see it to believe it" was not just a motto in my life—it was a *way* of life. People laughed at me because I always have to put my hands on things. I had to have proof before I would accept anything. It's been that way all through my life— the Easter Bunny and Santa Claus—ha! Couldn't fool me even when I was a kid. When it came time for the tooth fairy to make a visit, I wanted cash in my hand. Don't bore me with children's fantasies. When my mom and dad said they loved me, they had to back that up, if you know what I mean. When a young woman told me she loved me—no, I better not get into that.

You see, sometimes skepticism really has its benefits. But let me tell you, it has its downside too. To tell you the truth, being a skeptic has really hurt me as a person. I have a hard time believing anything. I'm so calculating sometimes that people can't even stand to be around me. People will tell me, "You should go over to this restaurant. They've got the best hamburgers in town." Sure. Or they say, "Did you see that new movie? It's the best movie ever." Sure again. Nothing is the best until me, Mr. Skeptic, puts his hands on it.

And I can't stand certain people. For instance, I'm just not the type of person who likes to hang around idealists. People like that are just "pie in the sky" people—too heavenly minded to be any earthly good in my book. It really bugs me. That's why it is not just odd but downright shocking that I would want to have anything to do with Jesus.

You can imagine what happened when one of my friends told me about Jesus. Two thousand years ago, miracles, risen from the dead—yeah, right. But then Jesus introduced Himself to me. And when Jesus introduced Himself to me, although I didn't want to believe, it was a big deal. I can't believe even today what I did—I sensed in my heart that He was looking at me. Although I didn't really fully understand it at the time, I decided I would follow Him. It's amazing, isn't it? That was the first time in my life that anything like that had ever happened. But I have to tell you, there is just something about Jesus. Even I, Mr. Skeptic, can't fully explain it. All I know is that there is a feeling in my heart that I've never experienced before.

You know, I heard about another guy named Thomas who, years ago, also followed Jesus. I heard that he was a guy just like me, a guy who needed proof. And you know, despite what it must have felt like to have actually known Jesus but still not believe Him, even when He's standing before your very eyes, it's just powerful—very powerful—to know that Jesus forgave him. Jesus just looked past Thomas's problem and said to him, "Look to Me." For some strange reason,

I feel Jesus saying the same thing to me. "Look to Me." You know, I can't fully explain it, but I know I've got to do that. In fact I *want* to do that! Maybe something's happening to me that even I, Mr. Tom Skeptic, would have a hard time believing could ever happen. And it's all because of Jesus. You see, my life has changed completely. (Written by Robin J. Dugall, 1996; to be used in conjunction with a message on Thomas or the theme of doubt or skepticism.)

Offering

Have students be the ushers for the offering time.

Closing Prayer

Either have a series of students pray or prepare a written prayer ahead of time that students can lead, like the following:

Leader 1: **Lord God, You have given us the opportunity and encouragement to pray for others. Hear our prayers as we lift people to You who need Your touch, love and healing.**

Leader 2: **For all Christian churches everywhere in the world. We pray that You'll bless these churches with Your grace, truth and power to bring the news of Jesus to everyone.**

People: **We bring this prayer to You, our great and loving Lord.**

Leader 1: **We pray for Christians everywhere in the world. We are brothers and sisters in the Body of Christ. We will be with each other worshiping You for eternity.**

Leader 2: **Bless all believers with a love for You and a passion to preach the gospel to all who need to know You.**

People: **We bring this prayer to You, our soon and coming King.**

Leader 1: **We pray for all people in our church who are sick or in some distress. We love them Lord and we know that You love them, too.**

Leader 2: **Give them strength, relief from suffering and the peace that only You can bring.**

People: **We bring this prayer to You, our merciful and gracious Savior.**

Leader 1: **Lord, we pray specifically for (insert specific prayer requests).**

Leader 2: **We thank You, Jesus, that You love us enough to give us the gift of prayer. We know You hear every prayer and act out of Your incredible love for each of us.**

People: **We praise You, Lord! Amen!**

Closing Music

Play music as the congregation leaves. Either play one of the students' favorite Christian CDs, or have students continue to sing songs from the service. **Note:** Some churches use creeds on a regular basis. Insert the creed as you need to or write one that has a student leader and congregational responses, such as the following:

Leader: **What do you believe?**

People: **I trust my life to God the Father, Creator of the Universe. He has made all that is and has given it to me as a gift of love. Despite how I rebel against Him, He continually seeks me that I might know true life in Him. I trust my life to God the Son, Jesus Christ, who became a human being like me, that I might know the love and forgiveness of God. He took my sins upon Him that His death might become my death to sin. He was raised to new life that His life might become my own, a gift through faith and trust in Him. I trust my life to God the Holy Spirit. He renews my life and recreates within me that once lost likeness of God. The Holy Spirit gathers me together with others and empowers me to do the work of Jesus in my world. I'll live my life in God, Father, Son and Holy Spirit, until He takes me into His arms to live forever. Amen.**

Note:
1. Jim Burns, gen. ed; Christine Stanfield and Joel Lusz, *Fresh Ideas: Skits & Dramas* (Ventura, CA: Gospel Light, 1998).

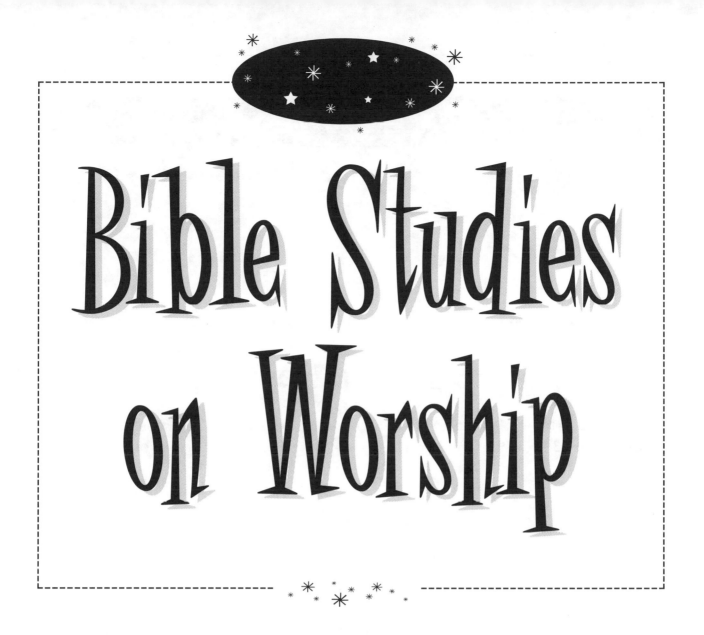

Bible Studies on Worship

Overview

Worship as a Priority

The Big Idea

Being a person of worship means being a devoted and maturing disciple of Jesus.

Biblical Basis

Psalm 40:8-10; 92:1,2; 95:6; Isaiah 6:1-4; 43:7; Romans 12:1,2; Ephesians 6:12; Colossians 3:16,17; 1 Thessalonians 5:16-18; 1 Peter 2:9; Revelation 5:11-14; 14:6,7

Objectives

During this study, you will guide students to:
- Understand that worshiping God needs to be a priority in their lives;
- Demonstrate the biblical principles of worship;
- Recognize that worship needs to be a foundational activity in their daily lives.

Preparation

- You will need Bibles, a white board, or overhead transparency and projector and the appropriate markers, 3x5-inch index cards and pens or pencils.
- Photocopy student handouts "Priorities" and "A Worship Covenant" (pp. 78-80).

Worship as a Priority

Warm-Up

What's Most Important

Begin your study with prayer and worship time; then read the following illustration:

> In the movie *Saving Private Ryan*, a graphic scene at the beginning of the film sets the emotional and dramatic tone of the entire movie. As the soldiers storm the Normandy beachhead on D day during World War II, they encounter horrendous gunfire from heavily entrenched Nazi soldiers overlooking the beach from the bluffs above. Soldiers are dying or being wounded so rapidly that it's horrifying.
>
> In the midst of the intense pressure and atmosphere of those moments, the main character, Captain Miller (played by Tom Hanks) correctly determines that the main priority of every soldier is to get off the beach and out of the line of fire. Under such severe circumstances, the soldiers' lives depend on a clear sense of purpose, direction and priority.

Explain: **Each of our lives is guided by priorities. No, we don't face the intensities that the troops encountered that day during World War II, but as Christians we do face the battle of life. In fact, in Ephesians 6:12 Paul says that we are at war with powers greater than ourselves whose main goal is to wipe us out. God says that unless we have firm God-honoring priorities, we can find ourselves far off the path of faithfulness.**

Team Effort

Priorities

Continue by explaining: **Priorities are things, values or aspects of your life that demand your attention. To prioritize your life means "to put things in order of their importance." We are going to take a few minutes to discuss priorities.**

- Divide students into small groups of three or four and distribute the "Priorities" hand-outs and pens or pencils to everyone.
- Allow 10 to 15 minutes for small groups to discuss the questions; then bring students back together to share some of their answers with the whole group.

In the Word

Our Priorities in Worship

- You will need Bibles and a white board or overhead transparency and projector and the appropriate markers.
- Ask volunteers to read the following Bible verses; then ask students to summarize what the priority is in each verse. Write their summaries on the white board or overhead transparency.

    Psalm 40:8-10 (To do God's will; proclaim His righteousness, love and truth)

    Psalm 92:1,2 (Praise the Lord; proclaim His love and faithfulness)

    Isaiah 6:1-4 (Declare His holiness and majesty; praise Him)

    Romans 12:1,2 (Offer our bodies as living sacrifices; be transformed by worship)

    Colossians 3:16,17 (Sing psalms, hymns and songs with gratitude to God)

    1 Thessalonians 5:16-18 (Be joyful always; pray continually; give thanks)

    Revelation 5:11-14 (Declare His worthiness; worship with praise, honor, glory and power)

Ask: **What do each of these passages have in common?** (Worship)

WHAT IS WORSHIP?

Discuss the following questions:

When you think of worship, what comes to mind?

If you could use another word for "worship," what would you use?

How do you worship best?

What gets your heart best prepared to encounter God? (Songs, prayer, silence, etc.)

What "shuts down" your worship? (Unconfessed sin, illness, distractions such as others talking, worries, being upset with parents or friends, having a bad day, etc.)

What sort of experiences derail you from being in touch with the Lord during worship? (Silence, songs, distractions, etc.)

WHAT IS GOD'S PURPOSE FOR US?

Using the following Bible verses as an outline to teach students about God's will for worship, explain: **From cover to cover, the Bible says that God wants His children to be worshipers. We are...**

Created to worship God (Read Isaiah 43:7);

Chosen by God to be worshipers (Read 1 Peter 2:9);

Called by God to be worshipers (Read Psalm 95:6);

Commanded by God to worship (Read Revelation 14:6,7).

Applying God's Truth

A Worship Covenant

- Distribute the "A Worship Covenant" handout, 3x5-inch index cards and pens or pencils.
- Allow 5 to 10 minutes for students to complete the handouts and write their worship covenants.
- Collect the index cards and place them in a pile. Pray over the cards, asking God to bless each of the commitments made before Him. Return the cards to the students, instructing them to keep their cards in their Bibles to remind them to worship and to guide their spiritual growth and accountability. **Note:** You might want to refer to the worship covenants again at a future meeting to ensure accountability.
- End the study with a song of worship and a time of prayer.

Priorities

This is an opportunity to share your faith *and* your struggles in worship with openness and honesty.

Remember, priorities are those things, values and activities that demand your attention. To prioritize your life means to put things in their order of importance.

Discuss the following:

1. What are the three top priorities in your life? Explain why they are in the order that you rank them.

   First

   Second

   Third

2. What do you think your parents would say *should* be your number-one priority? Why?

   What do you think your friends would say *should* be your number-one priority? Why?

   What do you think God would say *should* be your number-one priority?

3. How can you tell the priorities of another person?

   What do you spend most of your time doing every day?

   What does how you spend your time tell you about your priorities?

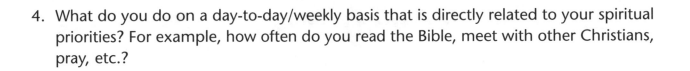

4. What do you do on a day-to-day/weekly basis that is directly related to your spiritual priorities? For example, how often do you read the Bible, meet with other Christians, pray, etc.?

   What do you think God would say about your spiritual priorities?

5. We can all improve on putting God first in our lives. None of us are perfect worshipers. What is one thing you can do to put God first in your life this coming week?

Ask the other small-group members to keep you accountable during the week by either phoning or talking to you at school. Pray for one another this week.

A Worship Covenant

Think about a typical day in your life.

1. What could you do to make worship a higher priority for you?

2. What do you already do to worship God?

3. What do you need to do to make worship a priority?

On the card provided, write out a plan for making a new commitment. Begin by writing:

> Dear Lord, without another moment's delay or hesitation, I make the following commitment to grow in my worship life with You. I dedicate this plan to You and I ask You to bless it. In Jesus' name, amen.

Then write out your plan, using the following suggestions:

- Determine a time of day that's right for you. Some people are morning people; some are evening people; some are just "out of it" all the time! What's a good time every day that you can spend in worship?
- Find a quiet place. Jesus went to a quiet place to pray—how about you? Where's a place that you won't be distracted in your worship?
- Be realistic. Don't say to yourself, *I'm going to worship for one hour every day.* Start small—even five minutes is a start. You can expand your time from there. Some days there will be more time to worship; other days there may be less time.
- Get some worship helps—CDs, devotional books, etc. Ask your youth leader for suggestions. Don't forget the most important item—your Bible!
- Consider writing out some of your prayers and keeping track of them in a journal or notebook. It will help keep you focused and give you an opportunity to see God's miraculous works in your life through your prayer and worship. It is a great help for future worship times as you read over past requests and praise Him for His answers and work in your life.

Sign and date your worship covenant and keep it in your Bible.

Overview

The Consequences of Worship

The Big Idea

When you worship, you put yourself in a position to allow God to change you!

Biblical Basis

Joshua 5:13,14; Psalm 22:3; 149:2-9; Isaiah 6:1-5; John 13:35; Acts 16:16-34; 2 Corinthians 3:18; Galatians 6:7; Colossians 3:12-17

Objectives

During this study, you will guide students to:
• Understand the power of worship;
• Demonstrate the biblical principle of worship;
• Expect things to happen in their lives when they worship.

Preparation

You'll need your Bible, photocopies of "Actions and Consequences" on page 86 and pens or pencils.

The Consequences of Worship

Warm–Up

Embarrassing Consequences

- Begin with prayer and worship, then read the following illustration. **Note:** Better yet, tell a story from from your life when you made a decision and faced difficult or interesting consequences as a result!

When I was in high school, I swam competitively. I had been swimming for years and was used to all the kidding that went along with long hours in the pool (that damaged my social life) and with the small bathing suits that swimmers had to wear. I remember when my mom first looked at a Speedo when I began swimming in eighth grade. She looked at that suit like she was looking at a magazine that was off-limits in our home.

After years of swimming, I grew accustomed to these suits and actually gained an appreciation for why a competitive swimmer would wear them. At one meet in my senior year, though, I got ready for a critical race and went to tighten the waistband on the suit when the cord in the band broke. Not worrying about it, I said to myself, *No problem; this suit is so tight and small, it will stay on without the cord.* So I pulled the broken cord out and got on the starting block.

When the starter's gun went off, I dove into the pool and started swimming. Suddenly I felt a strange sensation around my ankles. Yep, there in front of God and scores of cheering fans was my swimsuit. Not where it was supposed to be if you know what I mean. To say the least, I was embarrassed.

Team Effort

Actions and Consequences

Explain: **We all face consequences for our decisions and actions. That's a fact of life. Yet not all consequences have to be negative; there can be positive outcomes of the decisions we make and the actions we take.**

- Have students pair up and give each pair a copy of "Actions and Consequences". Instruct them to come up with at least two positive and two negative consequences of the actions listed on the handout.
- Ask each student to share with his/her partner about a time in their life when they did something that had a negative consequence and what they learned from that experience.
- Bring the whole group back together and continue: **Every decision you make has an impact on your life. That's true in every aspect of your life and it is especially true for your life in Jesus. Did you know that when you worship God, you face certain consequences? Let's learn about what those consequences are.**

In the Word

The Consequences of Worship

Explain: **Galatians 6:7 says, "You will always reap what you sow"** (*NLT*). **Although this truth from the Bible can be applied in many ways, God makes it very clear that the more you invest yourself in matters of the Spirit, the more you will get out of it. When it comes to worship, when you expect God to do something in your life, guess what will happen? He'll do it! If you invest yourself in the Lord, God says that you will see Him do things that will amaze you!**
   Some of the consequences of worship:

THE PRESENCE OF GOD
Read Psalm 22:3. Explain: **The Bible says that God is "enthroned" in the praises of His people. In other words, when we worship, God shows up!**
   Discuss:
   What happens when God shows up?
   If Jesus were to show up at your youth group meeting this week, what do you think He would want to do?

If Jesus met you personally today, what would He say and do in your life?

THE POWER OF GOD

Read the story of Paul and Silas in Acts 16:16-34. Explain: **The Bible says that when Paul and Silas were worshiping, God's power was released and they were set free. As a result, a person who did not know the Lord came to Christ. Someone was saved as a result of worship.**

Discuss:

Have you ever seen a person accept Christ?

Have you ever prayed with a person to accept Christ? What happened? How did you feel?

When you worship, do you sense God calling you to Himself? How?

How could the worship at our youth group or at our church be more evangelical, that is, more active in calling people to accept Jesus as Savior? How can that happen more?

LOVE AND UNITY AMONG CHRISTIANS

Read Colossians 3:12-17, then discuss:

In verse 14, how are Christians supposed to treat each other?

In verse 15, Paul tells us that there is a certain quality that should be obvious when Christians are "one body." What is that quality?

Continue: **In verses 16 and 17, Paul talks about worship. Worship is something that should draw us together as Christians and should be something that breaks down any barriers or problems that separate us as brothers and sisters in Jesus. In fact, Jesus says in John 13:35 that when Christians love each other, it is a visible sign to the world about the reality of God in their lives.**

Have you ever experienced a time of worship that drew you closer together with other Christians? Why would that happen?

OTHER CONSEQUENCES OF WORSHIP

- Have volunteers read the following verses; then have students discuss the additional consequences of true worship:

  Joshua 5:13,14—God makes His plans known.

  Psalm 149:2-9—God changes situations.

  Isaiah 6:1-5—God humbles us and His holiness convicts us of our sin.

  2 Corinthians 3:18—God's glory will be reflected and transform your life.

Applying God's Truth

- Have student pairs from the Team Effort each join another pair to form groups of four.

- Instruct students to share within their small groups one thing that each would like God to do in his or her personal life. Have students make a list of each request on the back of their "Actions and Consequences" handout.

- Remind students of the importance of respecting each other by keeping these requests among themselves; then have them pray together about the area that each member shared.

- Close this study by playing a simple worship song while the small groups hold hands, thanking God for how He wants to change our lives and trusting Him to do it.

- After a few minutes for small group prayer, have the whole group sing the worship song together.

Actions and Consequences

Brainstorm together at least two positive consequences and two negative consequences for each action.

Action	Positives	Negatives
Exercising regularly		
Not using a seatbelt		
Eating two double cheeseburgers every day		
Skipping school		
Using a credit card		
Being a loving and caring person		
Going to church regularly		
Getting three hours of sleep a night		
Failing to clean the cat box		
Kissing everybody you see at school		
Showering regularly		

Worship Exercises for Camps and Retreats

Usually, youth leaders are so concerned about food, the program agenda and other details at a camp or retreat that they neglect worship. Worship can be the most memorable aspect of the camp or retreat for students.

Camp Worship Booklet

Put together a student worship booklet for the week (or weekend) that has a mixture of Bible passages, questions for reflection and favorite songs that students could sing by themselves. This could be put together in a journal format allowing the students to take ownership over their own writing and devotional times for the week. After you begin every day of camp, give the students individual time to work on their worship journals. A good format for a camp worship journal would be the ACTS method with one day dedicated to each of the aspects of prayer and worship: Adoration, Confession, Thanksgiving, Supplication (p. 23). Encourage students to make these worship times a key part of their camp experience. See the "Sample Camp Worship Booklet" beginning on page 92.

Set Up a Camp Sanctuary

In addition to group worship times, find a cabin or a special spot on the property that will be a worship site for the week. Set it up with a boom box for soft music, a Bible, maybe some candles and a cross. You might want to put some of your favorite youth devotionals[1] in this spot. Tell students that this is their sanctuary for the week. It will be there for individual and small-group worship times that are not programmed in the camp's schedule.

Students should be able to access the worship spot only during the times that are not specifically planned by you and your team. Make a big deal about it. Tell students that you are going to spend time there during the week. Share stories at the end of the week about the special sanctuary. If a song, poem or special letter to God is written at the sanctuary, read it at group worship times. You can even call this place a hermitage and pass out stickers or pin-on buttons to those who have spent time there. Put "I am a hermit" on the sticker or button. The students will be blessed by this special worship place.

Have an Underground Service

This activity takes some planning, but it works great at camps and retreats where you have ample outdoor facilities. Throughout the week or weekend, inform students that there will be a secret worship service at the end of this time away from home. Explain that the location has not yet been decided, but they will hear more when the time is appropriate. Next, set up a worship site that is hidden in camp—either outdoors in the woods or in some location where the students have not had access during the week. This activity should be done in the dark to emphasize that worship is sometimes dangerous

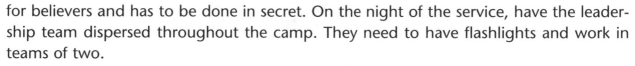

for believers and has to be done in secret. On the night of the service, have the leadership team dispersed throughout the camp. They need to have flashlights and work in teams of two.

Have all students meet in a common place and have the camp leader share with them that they are about to worship like early Christians—and those who still live in persecution—had to worship. Send the students out of the meeting place in pairs and have them walk from station to station following the flashlights of the teams that have been dispersed throughout the camp. Build some physical challenge into the path to the service. For example, if there is a small stream on the camp property, tie a rope across the stream and have a couple of leaders pull students across in a boat. After everybody arrives at the site, have a worship service and time for recommitment and/or dedication to the mission of the Lord. Talk about how important it is to follow the light of the Lord in the darkness of our world. This experience can be very effective if planned properly. Give it a try!

Invitation from God—A Special Communion Experience

Hand out the following letter personally addressed to every student at the camp. It requires preparation ahead of time, but in the end it is worth every minute. Plan this as a time of worship at the end of the camp. The day before the worship experience, hand each student an invitation, such as the following:

Dear Child of Mine,

You are officially invited by Me to a meal in your honor. You will be seated at the King's table and served by the King Himself. Please come as you are. Don't change on account of My presence; just come to Me. Bring an open heart and pure motives. We will commune together. When the bread is broken, I'll break it for you. When the wine is poured, I'll pour it for you. And when your burdens are lifted, it's because I have drawn near to take them from you. Sometimes, My children think that they need to do something during these important times with Me. Don't worry; you don't have to do a thing. Let Me serve you and let Me love you. This is the way that I meant it to be from the beginning. This is the way it is going to be for eternity—if you allow Me.

I love you, My child. Come!

Lovingly,

Jesus

Look to the Stars

During one of the evenings at camp, take the students out to a big field or an open spot in the camp facility. Have them lie on their backs in a huge circle with their heads toward the middle of the circle. Sing songs of worship. Then ask the students to begin to pray with their eyes open, looking at the stars. As they are praying, explain that just as there are innumerable stars in the heavens, so are God's thoughts of each of them. The Bible tells us that God's thoughts for every one of His children are so numerous that we cannot even begin to count them (see Psalm 40:5) and they outnumber the grains of sand (see Psalm 139:18). That's the extent of His love. God created this magnificent universe with each of us in mind. Worship is an opportunity for us to praise God for giving us the opportunity to enjoy His extravagance.

Get Wet

Cleansing and forgiveness are often paired together in the Bible. Take students to a lake or river or simply get a huge bowl of water. Have a time of worship with a confessional time. Ask the students to share with the Lord and with one other person the shortcomings and failures in their lives. Then, in pairs, have students get each other wet. While they are dunking or pouring some water on the heads of their friends, have them say the words, "The love of Jesus washes your sin away. Though your sins may be like scarlet, He makes you white as snow." (Remember, this is not baptism, but merely a symbolic act of the cleansing of sin.)

Silent Retreat

If you've never tried a silent retreat, you might want to try one just to see how it affects your students. Silence can be an amazing revealer of the depth of who we are. Try a silent retreat with adult leaders first, then the student leadership team and then the entire group. With a large group, have silent time periods. High school and junior high school students most likely will not be able to remain silent for an *entire* weekend. That's an understatement. Yet silent times with God need to be nurtured and taught. For a silent retreat, or period of time, have the group gather first for singing and group prayer. Instruct students on the benefits of silence in our lives. Give them a half hour of silence to start. Later in the weekend, try longer periods of time. Tell students that they can venture around the camp facilities; they simply cannot talk to anyone. If they run into someone, a wave or a simple hand gesture that you can agree on ahead of time can be a personal encouragement and greeting in the Lord.

Note:
1. Some suggested resources: Jim Burns, *Spirit Wings* (Ann Arbor, MI: Servant Publications, 1992); Max Lucado *In the Grip of Grace* (Nashville: Word Publishing, 1992); *He Still Moves Stones* (Word Publishing, 1993); *Just Like Jesus* (Word Publishing, 1998).

© 1999 by Gospel Light. Permission to photocopy granted. *Worship Experiences*

Camp Worship Booklet

Camp Worship Journal

GROWING IN GOD CHRIST'S LOVE

Introduction

Hi! I am your Camp Worship Book. As with any book, I am only good when I am used. So you have my permission to use me. What an offer! Seriously, I am being made available to you to enhance your growth and learning this week at camp. Enclosed in my pages are guidelines, maps if you will, on how your relationship with Jesus Christ can grow in dynamic ways. I want to expose you to the depths of God's love and power. Use me and you will grow. Follow my directions and you will be led by the Spirit of God into new heights of praise and service to the King. Hey, growth is the name of the game when you trust Jesus Christ with your life. Why not take advantage of what the Lord has to offer you? Go ahead; make my day—use me!

Types of Devotionals in My Pages

Journaling

This is like writing a diary. It's easy, but challenging. Take my advice: Be honest and open. Nobody is going to look at these pages except you. What do you have to lose? Read the instructions and begin writing. Don't hold back; let it all out—whatever crosses your mind and heart. Disciples of Jesus have been using journaling for centuries to record the movement of God in their lives. Go for it!

Quiet Time

These are guided times of reflection, helping you to see yourself and explore your feelings in relation to various Scripture passages and prayers. Remember, the Lord reveals Himself to you in many ways: through what you read, see, think and sense inside of you. Spend these quiet times being truly quiet and really listening to the Lord. You'll find them helpful if you do.

> May the words of my mouth and the meditation of my heart be pleasing in your sight, O Lord, my Rock and my Redeemer (Psalm 19:14).

Guided Personal Prayer

This week, you'll be learning about the **ACTS** method of prayer. Pastor Robin and many others use this as a simple way of guiding time spent with the Lord in prayer. It stands for "**A**doration, **C**onfession, **T**hanksgiving and **S**upplication," four parts of prayer that are essential for the maturing believer. Use this method this week. Train yourself to be a person of effective prayer.

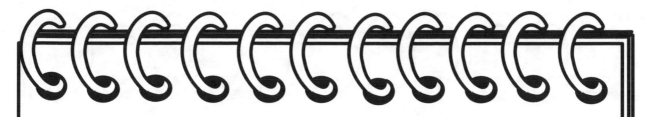

Morning Prayer

As morning breaks, I look to You,

O God, to be my strength this day.

Alleluia!

O God, You are my God,

For You my soul is thirsty.

My body pines for You,

Like a dry, weary land without water.

So I gaze upon You in Your sanctuary,

To see Your face and Your glory,

For Your love is better than life.

My lips shall sing Your praises.

I will bless You all the days of my life.

In Your name I will lift up my hands,

And my soul shall be filled, as with a banquet,

And my mouth shall praise You with joy.

As morning breaks, I look to You,

O God, to be my strength this day.

Alleluia!

—Adapted from Psalm 63

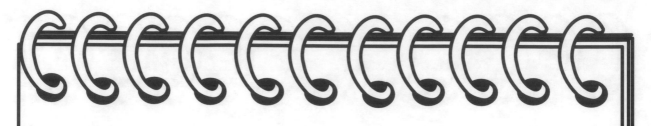

Afternoon Prayer

Lord, make me an instrument of Your peace.

Where there is hatred, let me sow love,

Where there is injury, pardon,

And where there is doubting, let me bring faith,

Lord, make me an instrument of Your peace.

Where there is despairing, hope,

Where there is darkness, Your light,

And where there is sadness, let me bring Your joy.

O Divine Master, grant that I might see

Not so much to be consoled, as to console,

To be understood, as to understand,

And not so much to be loved, as to love another.

For it is in giving that we now receive,

It is in pardoning that we are now pardoned,

And it is in dying that we are now born again.

Lord, make me an instrument of Your peace.

Where there is hatred let me bring You love.

—Prayer of St. Francis of Assisi,

Adapted by John Michael Talbot

The ACTS
Method of Prayer

Use the following as a guide in your personal prayer time through the week. You are encouraged to write out your prayers for each day during your quiet time.

Adoration—God, I praise You for being...

Confession—Lord, I confess the sin of...

Thanksgiving—God, I thank You for...

Supplication—Lord, today I pray for...

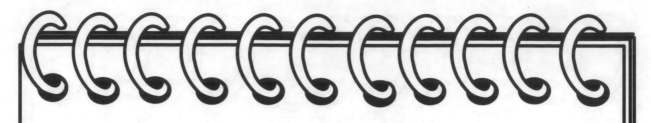

Spiritual Goals for the Day

Today I desire to do the following with:

- God

- My personal character as a Christian

- My friends

- My cabin

Day One Journaling

Instructions: Spend a few minutes in reflection and prayer about your relationship with Jesus Christ. Write any feelings in your journal. Draw a graph of your spiritual life so far.

For example:

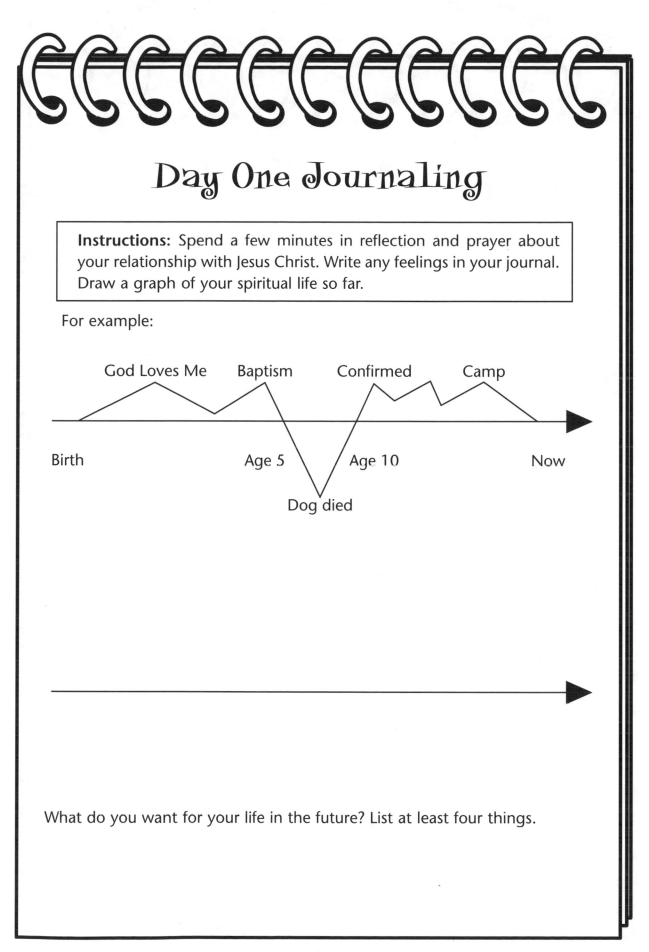

What do you want for your life in the future? List at least four things.

How will your relationship with Jesus Christ affect those things you want? List at least three or four ways.

How would you rate your commitment to Jesus on a scale of 1 to 10, with 10 being the highest?

Why did you rate yourself where you did on the scale?

Dream a little; how could your commitment deepen?

Before you continue, at the beginning of the week you will be assigned a Spiritual Director—someone from the staff who you will meet with one-on-one—and a Prayer Partner—someone who will pray for you and who you will pray intensely for this week. You will receive more information from the staff on each of these assignments, but for now, write their names here for your remembrance.

My Spiritual Director is _____.

Our meeting time and place is_____.

My Prayer Partner is _____.

Day Two Quiet Time

> **Instructions:** Begin by praying the Morning Prayer at the front of this journal.

Read Psalm 52.

Think about what God is doing in this psalm. What does "God's unfailing love" mean to you? How do you experience God's love?

How can you give thanks to God? Think of ways to give thanks to God. List them.

Use the rest of this page and the next, if needed, for your ACTS prayers for today. In addition, pray for today's sessions, your leaders, your friends and whatever else the Holy Spirit lays on your heart.

Day Two Journaling

God wants to break ground in your life today. That means that He wants to start to work in your life. He won't quit until He has brought you into the likeness of Jesus (see Philippians 1:6). What are some of the ways you feel God wants to break ground in your life?

Write the answers to the following in your journal: Who is Jesus? What is He like? What is His nature? What did He do? What were His habits? How did He act? What was His spiritual life like?

How do these facts about Jesus relate to you?

What is God going to have to do and change in your life to make you more like Jesus?

Day Three
Quiet Time, Part I

> **Instructions:** Begin by praying the Morning Prayer at the beginning of this journal.

Read Psalm 78:7,8.

How much confidence do you have in God? Do you want to put more confidence in Him?

Read Philippians 1:6.

How has God been faithful to you in your life?

Do you feel like He's never going to give up on you? How does God communicate that promise to you? Write your thoughts and any other thoughts about what God is teaching you at this time.

Use the rest of this page to write out your ACTS prayers for today. Remember, God answers prayers and loves you deeply—so deeply that your concerns move His heart.

Day Three Journaling

Reflect and pray about the day that you have experienced so far. Read Romans 7:14-25. Imagine the battle going on within you.

What *is* going on inside of you? What war is being waged? What are the growing pains you are experiencing as a Christian?

What is the easiest aspect of being a disciple of Jesus Christ?

What is the most difficult aspect of being a disciple of Jesus Christ?

Jesus calls you to be obedient to Him. What does being obedient to God mean to you?

Are you going to have to give something up in order to be obedient? What might you have to give up? (If you're not sure, ask God to reveal it to you.)

Day Three
Quiet Time, Part II

Before Bed

> **Instructions:** Begin by praying the Afternoon Prayer at the beginning of this journal.

Read Psalm 4:1-5.

How has God answered prayer in your life?

What sacrifices do you offer to the Lord?

How has God answered your prayers today?

Has your Prayer Partner for the week been blessed? How about other people on your prayer list?

Spend the rest of your quiet time thinking and reflecting about the Lord. Try saying the name of Jesus over and over again in a whisper. Write any thoughts that you have. Fall asleep in the Lord's peace.

Day Four Quiet Time

Instruction: Begin your time with the Morning Prayer.

Read Psalm 139.

What do these verses mean to you?

How does it feel to be so wonderfully handmade by the Lord?

What can that mean for your life? Write down what you are thinking and feeling.

Use the rest of this page for your ACTS prayer time.

Day Four Journaling

Reflect and pray about the topic for today.

How are you blossoming for the Lord?

What does discipleship mean to you?

How can you be a more committed disciple of Jesus?

Write down two or three things you can do to grow in the following areas:

• Fellowship with other Christians

• Worship

• Sharing Christ with others

• Sacrificial living

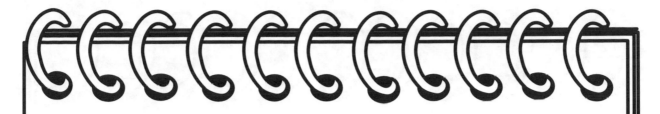

In terms of your growth in Jesus, how would you share your faith if someone asked you about your trust in God? Write down what you would share with a person about who Jesus is and what He means to you.

Day Five Quiet Time

Instructions: Begin by praying the Afternoon Prayer.

Read Psalm 91:1-11.

What has God promised to us for our protection?

If you could visualize the "shelter of the Most High," what would it look, feel and sound like?

How does it feel to know that the Lord gives His angels to "guard you in all your ways"?

In what specific areas do you need the Lord's protection?

Write out your ACTS prayers for the day.

Day Five Journaling

Reflect and pray about today's topic.

How does all this information about God's power strike you? Do you feel powerless to do all that Jesus wants you to do?

Who specifically do you think God would like to touch through you?

Who could He heal?

Who could He comfort?

Who could He save?

Make a list of people in your life who need something powerful from the Lord. List each person and his or her need.

What could you do about each need?

Day Six Quiet Time

Last One at Camp!

> **Instructions:** Begin by praying both prayers at the beginning of this journal.

Read Psalm 150.

What aspects of God's nature bless you? His love? Forgiveness? Mercy? Knowledge of you? Holiness? Praise God in prayer for His nature.

What can you praise God for this week? List some things you want to praise God for. For example: friends, the way the Lord has ministered to you, music, quiet times, food and anything else you can think of—you are blessed every-*day* in every*thing* through Him.

Spiritual Strategy

List three things you can do when you return home to continue to be all that Jesus calls you to be as His disciple.

1.

2.

3.

A Final Word

With the completion of Day Six Quiet Time, you have completed your week at camp. The lessons you have learned are not just important, but vital to your maturing life in Christ. One of the lessons experienced this week has to do with this journal. It provides you with a great model for future times with the Lord. You are encouraged to keep praying, reflecting on and journaling your walk with Jesus. As you do, you will grow.

Suggested Reading

Periodicals

Worship Leader. Nashville: CCM Communications 1-800-286-8099. A monthly magazine packed with helpful articles ranging from leading worship to sound and musical equipment to reviews of new worship materials and resources. This magazine is a must for every worship leader!

Books

Boschman, LaMar. *Future Worship.* Ventura, CA: Renew Books, 1998. A timely book that addresses the importance of passionate worship in connecting with our heavenly Father in the most intimate way.

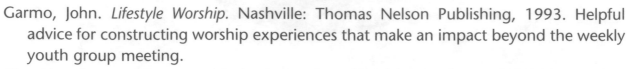

Garmo, John. *Lifestyle Worship.* Nashville: Thomas Nelson Publishing, 1993. Helpful advice for constructing worship experiences that make an impact beyond the weekly youth group meeting.

Gire, Ken. *Intense Moments with the Savior.* Grand Rapids: Zondervan Publishing House, 1992. A biblical devotional that focuses on the life of Jesus that guides you to read, envision and pray through the events of Jesus' ministry. This book will help you in the much-needed application process of Scripture to daily living for your students; an excellent resource for building a leader's heart for Jesus.

———. *Intimate Moments with the Savior.* Grand Rapids: Zondervan Publishing House, 1992. A biblical devotional focusing on Jesus' responses to the people closest to Him. Contains great ideas on how to take the Bible and work with it in a worshipful manner.

———. *Windows of the Soul: Experiencing God in New Ways.* Grand Rapids: Zondervan Publishing House, 1996. A refreshing devotional book that encourages the reader to look at daily events as they reveal the presence of God and the meaning of life in Jesus. An excellent resource book for devotional readings.

Hayford, Jack W. *Worship His Majesty.* Waco, TX: Word Publishing, 1987. This is a Bible study focusing on the effects of worship in the lives of key Old Testament figures. A classic ahead of its time, this book encourages us to lead, facilitate and plan life-changing worship experiences.

Kendrick, Graham. *Learning to Worship As a Way of Life.* Minneapolis: Bethany House Publishing, 1984. Written by one of the leading composers of contemporary worship music, this is an excellent book to build a worship leader's heart for God.

Mains, David. *Putting God in His Place.* Nashville: Star Song Publishing Group, 1994. A valuable book that illustrates the main themes of any great worship experience: praise, celebration, reflection on the ministry of Jesus and taking the worship experience into our daily lives as we serve and love people in the name of Jesus.

Marion, Jim. *Leading Your Students in Worship.* Wheaton, IL: Victor Books, 1993. A practical "how to" for putting together worship experiences for a youth ministry.

———. *Worship Services for Youth Groups.* Grand Rapids: Zondervan Publishing House, 1996. Outlining 12 worship experiences for youth ministry, this book is helpful in illustrating how a creative worship experience can be planned.

Morgenthaler, Sally. *Worship Evangelism.* Grand Rapids: Zondervan Publishing House, 1995. This new textbook on contemporary evangelical worship explores the whys and hows of worship in an in-depth and biblically sound manner.

Roberts, Francis. *Come Away, My Beloved.* Ojai, CA: King's Farspan, Inc., 1973. One of the classics in Christian devotional literature, this volume speaks to the reader as if God were speaking directly to the heart, encouraging the reader to allow God to speak in and through worship.

Webber, Robert. *The Worship Phenomenon.* Nashville: Abbott Martyn Publishing, 1994. Robert Webber is a pioneer in bringing together the best traditional and contemporary expressions of worship. Provides ideas, theological principles and practical advice on worship experiences, not only ministering to students, but bridging the gap between generations as well.

Wright, Tim and Jan. *Contemporary Worship.* Nashville: Abingdon Press, 1997. Although this book is meant for congregational application, it can be helpful in planning worship experiences for youth ministry as well, including suggestions on subjects ranging from music selection to preaching.

Yaconelli, Michael. *Dangerous Wonder.* Colorado Springs: Navpress Books, 1998. A veteran youth worker shares how to recapture the wonder of innocence of childhood and apply it to a relationship with God. A "freeing" book, it helps the youth worker realize the awe and wonder that comes from the adventure of faith.

Zschech, Darlene. *Worship.* Australia: Hillsongs Australia Leadership Series, 1996. A recognized composer and worship leader with Hills Christian Life Center in Australia, Darlene Zschech opens her heart about leading worship and worship teams.

Note:
The publishers do not necessarily endorse the entire contents of all publications referred to in this manual.

Add a New Member to Your Youth Staff.

Jim Burns is president of the National Institute of Youth Ministry.

Meet Jim Burns. He won't play guitar and he doesn't do windows, but he will take care of your programming needs. That's because his new curriculum, **YouthBuilders Group Bible Studies**, is a comprehensive program designed to take your group through their high school years. (If you have junior high kids in your group, **YouthBuilders** works for them too.)

For less than $6 a month, you'll get Jim Burns' special recipe of high-involvement, discussion-oriented, Bible-centered studies. It's the next generation of Bible curriculum for youth—and with Jim on your staff, you'll be free to spend more time one-on-one with the kids in your group.

Here are some of Youth-Builders' hottest features:

- Reproducible pages—one book fits your whole group
- Wide appeal—big groups, small groups—even adjusts to combine junior high/high school groups
- Hits home—special section to involve parents with every session of the study
- Interactive Bible discovery—geared to help young people find answers themselves
- Cheat sheets—a Bible *Tuck-In*™ with all the session information on a single page
- Flexible format—perfect for Sunday mornings, midweek youth meetings, or camps and retreats
- Three studies in one—each study has three four-session modules that examine critical life choices.

   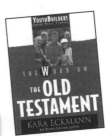 

12 Books in the Series!

The Word on Sex, Drugs & Rock 'N' Roll
ISBN 08307.16424 $16.99

The Word on Prayer and the Devotional Life
ISBN 08307.16432 $16.99

The Word on the Basics of Christianity
ISBN 08307.16440 $16.99

The Word on Being a Leader, Serving Others & Sharing Your Faith
ISBN 08307.16459 $16.99

The Word on Helping Friends in Crisis
ISBN 08307.16467 $16.99

The Word on the Life of Jesus
ISBN 08307.16475 $16.99

The Word on Finding and Using Your Spiritual Gifts
ISBN 08307.17897 $16.99

The Word on the Sermon on the Mount
ISBN 08307.17234 $16.99

The Word on Spiritual Warfare
ISBN 08307.17242 $16.99

The Word on the New Testament
ISBN 08307.17250 $16.99

The Word on the Old Testament
ISBN 08307.17269 $16.99

The Word on Family
ISBN 08307.17277 $16.99

More Great Resources from Jim Burns

Drugproof Your Kids
Stephen Arterburn and Jim Burns

Solid biblical principles are combined with the most effective prevention and intervention techniques to give parents a guide they can trust.
ISBN 08307.17714 $10.99

Drugproof Your Kids Video
A 90-minute seminar featuring Stephen Arterburn and Jim Burns. Includes a reproducible syllabus.
SPCN 85116.00876 $19.99

Parenting Teens Positively
Video *Featuring Jim Burns*

Understand the forces shaping the world of a teenager and what you can do to be a positive influence. This powerful message of hope is for anyone working with—or living with—youth. Includes reproducible syllabus. UPC 607135.000655 $29.99

Surviving Adolescence
Jim Burns

Jim Burns helps teens—and their parents—negotiate the path from adolescence to adulthood with real-life stories that show how to make it through the teen years in one piece. ISBN 08307.20650 $9.99

For these and more great resources and to learn about NIYM's leadership training, call **1-800-397-9725.**

Gospel Light

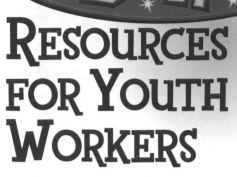

RESOURCES FOR YOUTH WORKERS

Jim Burns, General Editor

Turn your youth group meetings into dynamic, exciting events that kids look forward to attending week after week! Supercharge your messages, grab their attention with your activities and connect with kids the first time and every time with these great resources. Just try to keep these books on the shelf!

ILLUSTRATIONS, STORIES AND QUOTES TO HANG YOUR MESSAGE ON

Few things get your point across faster or with greater impact than a memorable story with a twist. Grab your teens' attention by talking with your mouth full of unforgettable stories.
Manual, ISBN 08307.18834 $16.99

CASE STUDIES, TALK SHEETS AND DISCUSSION STARTERS

Teens learn best when they talk—not when you talk at them. A discussion allowing youth to discover the truth for themselves, with your guidance, is a powerful experience that will stay with them for a lifetime.
Manual, ISBN 08307.18842 $16.99

GAMES, CROWDBREAKERS AND COMMUNITY BUILDERS

Dozens of innovative, youth-group-tested ideas for fun and original crowdbreakers, as well as successful plans and trips for building a sense of community in your group.
Manual, ISBN 08307.18818 $16.99

More Resources for Youth Workers, Parents & Students

Steering Them Straight
Stephen Arterburn & Jim Burns

Parents can find understanding as well as practical tools to deal with crisis situations. Includes guidelines that will help any family prevent problems before they develop.
UPC 156179.4066 $10.99

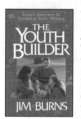

The Youth Builder
Jim Burns

This Gold Medallion Award winner provides you with proven methods, specific recommendations and hands-on examples of handling and understanding the problems and challenges of youth ministry.
ISBN 089081.1576. $16.95

Spirit Wings
Jim Burns

In the language of today's teens, these 84 short devotionals will encourage youth to build a stronger and more intimate relationship with God.
ISBN 08928.37837 $10.95

Radical Love
Book & Video, Jim Burns

In *Radical Love* kids discover why it's best to wait on God's timing, how to say no when their bodies say yes and how to find forgiveness for past mistakes.
Paperback, ISBN 08307.17935 $9.99
VHS Video, SPCN 85116.00922 $19.99

90 Days Through the New Testament
Jim Burns

A growth experience through the New Testament that lays the foundation for developing a daily time with God.
ISBN 08307.14561 $9.99

Getting in Touch with God
Jim Burns

Develop a consistent and disciplined time with God in the midst of hectic schedules as Jim Burns shares with you inspiring devotional readings to deepen your love of God.
ISBN 08908.15208 $2.95

Radical Christianity
Book & Video, Jim Burns

Radical Christianity is a proven plan to help youth live a life that's worth living and make a difference in their world.
Paperback, ISBN 08307.17927 $9.99
VHS Video, SPCN 85116.01082 $19.99

The Youth Worker's Book of Case Studies
Jim Burns

Fifty-two true stories with discussion questions to add interest to Bible studies.
ISBN 08307.15827 $12.99

To order NIYM resources, please call
1-800-397-9725
or to learn how you can take advantage of NIYM training opportunities call or write to:
NIYM • PO Box 297 • San Juan Capistrano
CA 92675 • 949/487-0217

What in the world is *NIYM*?

A.) The Neurotically Inclined Yo-Yo Masters
B.) The Neatest Incidental Yearbook Mystery
C.) The Natural Ignition Yields of Marshmallows
D.) The National Institute of Youth Ministry

If you deliberately picked A, B, or C you're the reason Jim Burns started NIYM! If you picked D, you can go to the next page. In any case, you could learn more about NIYM. Here are some IQ score-raisers:

Jim Burns started NIYM to:
• Meet the growing needs of training and equipping youth workers and parents
• Develop excellent resources and events for young people—in the U.S. and internationally
• Empower young people and their families to make wise decisions and experience a vital Christian lifestyle.

NIYM can make a difference in your life and enhance your youth work skills through these special events:

Institutes—These consist of week-long, in-depth small-group training sessions for youth workers.

Trainer of Trainees—NIYM will train you to train others. You can use this training with your volunteers, parents and denominational events. You can go through the certification process and become an official NIYM associate. (No, you don't get a badge or decoder ring).

International Training—Join NIYM associates to bring youth ministry to kids and adults around the world. (You'll learn meanings to universal words like "yo!" and "hey!')

Custom Training—These are special training events for denominational groups, churches, networks, colleges and seminaries.

Parent Forums—We'll come to your church or community with two incredible hours of learning, interaction and fellowship. It'll be fun finding out who makes your kids tick!

Youth Events—Dynamic speakers, interaction and drama bring a powerful message to kids through a fun and fast-paced day. Our youth events include: This Side Up, Radical Respect, Surviving Adolescence and Peer Leadership.

For brain food or a free information packet about the National Institute of Youth Ministry, write to:

NIYM
P.O. Box 297 • San Juan Capistrano, CA 92675
Tel: (949) 487-0217 • Fax: (949) 487-1758 • Info@niym.org